Adventures of the Saltwater Cowboy

~ a collection of "creative" non-fiction short stories

Jon Edward Edwards

Published by Simon Publishing LLC ®
Simon Publishing LLC is a registered trademark.
  https://www.simonpublishingllc.com/

ISBN: 979-8-9894345-6-5
Library of Congress Control Number: 2024910982

Cover Design:
Photo by Jennifer L. Cloud

Graphic Design by:
  Daphne McLeod
  Rick Ricozzi
  Melissa Waters

Interior Photos by:
  Jon Edward Edwards
  Daphne McLeod (*Hoot Owl* photos)

Interior Artwork by Jon Edward Edwards

Interior Graphic Design by Melissa Waters

Printed by Ingram Spark
First Edition
2 0 2 4 0 6 0 1

Dedication

To my son, **Will Edwards**. I wouldn't be who I am today if not for you. You're a beacon of light guiding me through tough times. Your stalwart attitude, positivity, and resilience lift my spirit and inject me with strength and courage. Thank you for being there for me every single day. This one is for you, Bubba.

Adventures of the Saltwater Cowboy

– a collection of "creative" non-fiction short stories

Jon Edward Edwards

Simon Publishing LLC

SIMON PUBLISHING

Contents

Adventures of the Saltwater Cowboy

Acknowledgments 1

Foreword 9

1. 10,000 Islands Paradox 19
2. Good Morning, Camper 22
3. Coming in Hot 27
4. How Many Wraps 31
5. When You Can 34
6. Debunked Banana 37
7. Purple Fade 40
8. Hoot Owl 42
9. Looking a Little Green 47
10. Spring Tide Rock Pile 50
11. Ride the Lightning 54
12. Beavertail Sandwich 58
13. White Pelicans 62
14. Hold on Loosely 64
15. Knife to a Gun Fight 69
16. Flip Flop 74
17. He's Doing It Again 78
18. 10,000 Islands Christmas 82
19. Well, Do You Feel Lucky? 86
20. Redtile Dysfunction 91
21. How Dare You 95
22. Four on Five 100
23. Nice Gainer 105
24. Salesman of the Year 110
25. Ride It Out 113
26. Biggest Fan 117
27. Hooked 123
28. Ditch City 128
29. Lake Claiborne Fire Drill 137
30. Past the First Bridge 140
31. You've Been Documented 152

Contents

Capt. Max Dean Novel Previews

Beautiful Day

1. Black Creek 165
2. Caloosa Island Marina 178

DEAD RIVER

1. Patient A'hole 197
2. Dead River 204
3. Nightmare in Olga 216

Acknowledgments

Dr. Martin Luther King said the measure of a man isn't where he stands in moments of convenience and comfort but where he stands at times of challenge and controversy. Plato felt the gauge of character is what a person does with power. Others say it's not how much one has but how much they give. I read a list of thirty "Measure of a Man" quotes, and none said, "The measure of a man is relative to the quality of the friendships and relationships he has amassed." I said that.

I stand stalwart in challenge and controversy because the seats for convenience and comfort are always taken. Perhaps that is due to my disability, "Acute Punctual Syndrome," an unfortunate condition that should qualify me for some government assistance. I'm in the middle of an exhausting and probably impossible task of having my diagnosis registered with the Medical Society That Registers Stuff. Nowadays, mental health is carrying less of a stigma, and things are changing. But no one wants to hear, "I just couldn't make it on time."

However, my cup overfloweth with positive karma and powerful mojos. My Amigos provide that convenience and comfort, the emotional accoutrement that even staunch loners require.

First and foremost, I'd like to thank **Daphne McLeod**, my small in stature yet large in life mother. I could write volumes of material describing the ways she's helped me. Any method of assistance you can think of, she did.

My stepdad, **Bob** (he spells it backward), a huge proponent, frequent proofreader, supporter, and sometimes sponsor, deserves substantial credit.

Jesse Dawson is what we call back home a "good shit." Thanks to Jesse, 2020 was my chance to be a writer, as I lived in Jesse's house, paid the yard guy, and took care of Vladimir for the better part of a year while I wrote.

My little bro, **Captain Drake Noble**, a fellow fiction aficionado, wise beyond his years, became my first proofreader. He was as good at pumping me up as he was tearing me down; he's the only friend who encouraged me without a nudge and among the few I can bounce things off.

Jennifer Edwards, my stepmom, is responsible for getting my foot in the door of the Everglades City Mullet Rapper by introducing me to **Kathy Brock** and, subsequently, **Val Simon** and **Lynn Alexander** with the Marco Island Coastal Breeze—six hundred to eight hundred words on the 10,000 Islands they wanted. I started cranking them out. Jennifer, please tell **Ronnie** thanks for the story fodder.

Lynn and **Val** deserve another credit for their steadfast support, and **Lynn** for proofreading. **Deborah Daniels**, don't think I forgot about you and the years of support and proofreading you've done. Thank you. I would be remiss not to mention the **Marco Island Writers Guild** and thank everyone for their steadfast help and encouragement.

Ashley Elston, congratulations on the NY Times Bestseller – First Lie Wins! Ashley has been my writing "Big Sis" (even though I'm nearly a year older) and advisor since shortly after I realized I had some natural talent and chose to pursue it. In 2015, she gave me the most significant compliment I'd received when she said I have a unique ability to tell a story in a few words, to get in and out, and how difficult it is to evoke emotion that quick. Hmm…, The long form is more difficult for me. Around that time, she encouraged me to find a home for my short stories. Which is what I did, although it took five long years.

My namesake, not former Louisiana Governor Edwin Edwards, but my uncle, **Dr. Jon L. Gibson**, has been a significant influence since the beginning. A renowned archaeologist, five-time author, and accomplished artist/illustrator, I'm proud to have inherited some of his creativity. Thank you for your tutelage.

Aunt Mary Beth, thank you for your support and the proofreading. To the rest of the Haynesville contingent, **Erin, Piper, and Lark**, thank y'all for your support over the years.

I would be remiss (never live it down) not to give a special thanks to my cousin, **Blair Sherman**, whose encouragement and brutal honesty I've counted on along the way – no shit. **Mark Locke**, you bet I didn't forget all your proofreading. Thank you, Amigo. And keep writing.

Aunt Jerrie, thank you for your staunch support.

Before I was published, I posted the occasional piece on social media. One day, Mom and Bob's Chapel Hill friend (by way of Lake Charles, Louisiana), champion mojo-pumper **Gordon Nixon**, replied to my post, "Another adventure of the Saltwater Cowboy." Bam! It's not cool to nickname yourself, it has to be organic, or it's bullshit.

Thank you, **Gordo & Eileen, Farely & Roger**, and the rest of the Chapel Hill Contingent for your support. Specifically, Photographer **Rick Ricozzi** (R.I.P.) posthumously for photoshopping the poling platform out of the way of the Cape Romano Dome Houses in the original photo used for the cover. The platform, standard on flats boats, mounted above the outboard motor, is used by traditional flats guides to pole their anglers in position. It obscured the view to the point of worthlessness. Credit to **Jenny Lindsey** for taking the pic and creating the scenario that blessed us with Rick and his magic. Thanks to Daph for the artistic rendering.

Jenny. You helped me through some of my darkest moments and remain a bright spot in my sometimes troubled mind. I admire your strength and ability to persevere.

Thank you to my publishing team. **Joanne Tailele** and **Melissa Waters** are working on the manuscript as I write.

Much love to my core group in Monroe, a merry band closer than brothers and sisters: **Sperry, Osama Ben Hajjin, Heath, Woods, Hill, Barney, Blair, Clint, Hopper, Hawsey, Hebert, the Jims, Staab, Bershen, Ryno, Trampus, Amy, Nici,** and the **Greco Twins**.

Hattiesburg Faction: **Jason, Andrew, Rob, Big Byrd, Peanut, Jane Clair, Bowman, Yancy, Darren,** and **Cameron**. Love to you all. Shout out to Team Beautiful Day: **Millard, Andrew, Corn**, our Captain, **Brian Broom**, and "sometimes" resident Alva pro, **Bill Danforth**. I don't know how I packed a lifetime's worth of memories and amassed the friendships I have in only two short years. It is a testament to the area and the people.

Naples Family: **Drake, Dock, and Jama, Capt. Joel and Kimmy, Heger, Capt. Ray** and **Gloma** – the fisherman in the family. **Tony B., Tom O., M. F. B.**, and the **Trailer Crew** – you know who you are. **Lucky, Brian G., Tiny, Greg O., George, Jim S., D.J.**, and **Brother Dave**. Thank y'all for being y'all and gracing me with your friendship.

Thank you to my **Facebook** and **Insta followers** who read the material force-fed them for a decade before I talked someone (Kathy Brock and Val Simon) into publishing my stories.

Adventures
of the
Saltwater Cowboy

Foreword

I got shock treatment, did a stint in rehab, got divorced, and started writing. I haven't stopped. Besides two brief "girlfriends" who only furthered my soured stance on sanctity, I've had nothing to distract me, professional career and time with my son notwithstanding. I believe in the 10,000-hour rule. If my math is correct, I'll be a master at my craft by the time I'm 56. Keep in mind that I hadn't picked a pen up until 2009.

What you have before you is the total of my published work since I found an outlet - The Marco Island Coastal Breeze and the Everglades City Mullet Rapper. Also included are samples of two novels that I'm excited about.

Why should you care? Because my life and imagination are wild, and some say I have a unique ability to tell stories and make them up with my fingers. These stories have graced the pages of the Coastal Breeze and the Mullet Rapper since 2020. The Breeze, that local rag you see in every resort community in the restaurants, drugstores, convenience stores, parks, and bus stops – they're everywhere. Yet, I do not know how many people pick up and read them. I get no response from the online versions as well. But Lynn, Val, and Kathy keep printing them.

I've lived a high-octane life, residing in every coastal state along the Gulf of Mexico Rim by the time I was fifteen, aside from Alabama, which, let's face it, was shafted when the U.S. government delved out the original Florida counties to make the state.

Let there be no mistake: Florida is my adopted home. I knew I belonged here since I was seventeen years old. That said, my heart will always belong to the *Sportsman's Paradise—the* only state in the union with a completely different set of laws - the *Napoleonic Code*. We don't have counties - we have parishes. We like our politicians shady, our levees substandard, and our food spicy. Hailing from Louisiana inflates my outdoor pedigree. For Rednecks, Louisiana is the outdoorsman's Harvard.

Regarding shady politicians and Louisiana, one cold winter's morning in '74, sitting in a steel pit blind sunken in a levee between two flooded rice fields, thousands of decoys shaking in the breeze, Ronnie, my dad, told a friend of then Governor Edwin Edwards, that he named his only son after the infamous Louisiana politician. He didn't. Mom named me after my uncle, renowned archaeologist and author Dr. Jon Gibson.

Word got back to the Governor, and a few months later, I was on the steps of the Homer, Louisiana courthouse receiving an honor – Master Jon Edward Edwards, Colonel on the Governor's Staff. I got my picture in the paper and a plaque and everything. All over a ruse that

Governor Edwards, finally going down in 2002 for rack-
eteering, would have appreciated more than anyone.

The event with Governor Edwards is a testament
to the uniqueness of our state and an example of the message in many of these stories, fraudulent nature notwithstanding. Relationships built on the water and in the field
forge bonds that transcend typical interaction.

My life was destined to be interesting, and I hit
the water swimming. Like a Labrador Retriever, I just
knew how. *"The next thing he will say is that he has
webbed feet,"* one may say. No, I don't, but two friends
from North Louisiana have webbed toes. And here go the
inbred jokes.

We moved to Texas shortly after I was born until
I was five years old, where I caught a ten-pound carp on
a Mickey Mouse Zebco on Lake Texoma and rode dirt
bikes in the hills and dunes around Grapevine. In 1980,
we relocated to Louisiana, the northeast part of the state,
Monroe. For the next two years, I could be found somewhere along the Ouachita River on a yellow Yamaha GT
80. A washed-out section of Indian mounds called Ooga
Ooga Land comes to mind.

Aside from living with Ronnie in Mississippi for two years and Tampa for half a year, the Chauvin River Basin on the north side of Monroe, Louisiana, would become my playground until I graduated college and left North Louisiana for good in '96. But not without a heavy heart.

There can't be many places left that offer such outdoor freedom. A sportsman's nirvana: Bayou Desaird, the Ouachita River, the river basin, and its bar pits, my friends and I engaged in a lifetime of adventure within approximately four square miles.

Thomas and I wakeboarding at first light on the Bayou during summertime was like skating on black ice. Water dead calm and dark from the alluvial soil of the river delta, spray erupting like shattered glass as you cut across the wake.

In Spring, after the first significant rain inundated the bar pits and receded, we'd tow a small jon boat behind Hill's four-wheeler behind the levee and deep into the basin where white perch were trapped in the bar pits and hungry. In the same pits, we caught crawfish using nets rimmed with wire. Baited with turkey necks, we used a long stick to reach out into the deepest parts of the depression to set the nets.

In chest waders, we hunted wood ducks in the flooded timber behind Ned's house, fog rising off the water, trying to shield our faces from the freshly migrated blue and green wing teal and native wood ducks. Ole' Ned taught me two valuable lessons among sportsmen after I returned his Browning BPS in a condition lesser than I'd borrowed it - a story itself. It involves falling into the pit blind at the LA-Ark Hilton - Big Sperry's camp in Jones.

Moving around as a kid sucked, and I dealt with the anxiety by attracting attention. I come from a long line of gifted, funny people, and I discovered I had a knack for making people laugh early on, telling jokes, flinging movie quotes with impeccable timing, and making impressions. Unbeknownst to me, I was writing bits. Every instance required creative thought and focus through execution, pass or fail, crickets or kill.

Such as the legend at Louisiana Tech University (Kappa Sigma – Epsilon Gamma) about a man they called "Porkchop," a physical comedian who would show up at random in various stages of undress, primarily complete. Aside from his trademark pull-on Redwing Work Boots and a hat – sometimes.

Eyewitness accounts say this character exhibited no inhibitions, performing a routine that had the crowd on the floor every time. Sometimes, he'd walk into a party and mingle, order a drink, turn around, and face the public while he waited as if he wasn't al-fresco.

I've heard bits and pieces – rumors – over the years that this person is me. I can neither confirm nor deny these accusations. However, should there be any truth to it, let it be known that I own creative license.

I've caught ten-pound bass on Lake Fork, Texas, jerked white perch from run-offs on Davis Island with cane poles, caught Opelousas catfish on trot-lines in the Mississippi River, pulled Spiney Tail Lobster from haunts shared with moray eels in the Keys, and hunted quail on horseback in the Plains of North, Texas. Following the noses of bird dogs along a ridge overlooking the Peace River, I could hear the lyrics of a George Strait song in my head:

> *When that sun is high in that Texas sky*
> *I'll be bucking it to County Fair*

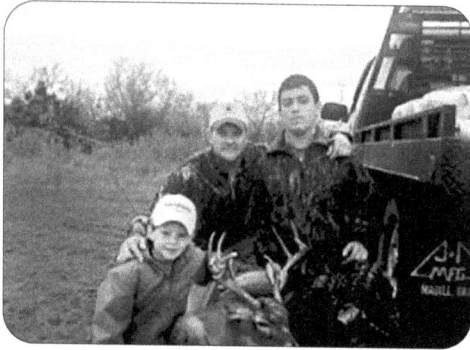

Paducah, Texas, a place near and dear to my heart, where Boone and Crockett Trophy whitetail deer roamed the natural gulleys, and wild Eastern and Rio-Grande gobblers roosted in the buttonwoods on the edge of the river pasture. Home of the Running R Ranch, where I watched Ronnie ride a bucking quarter horse from one stable to another, separated by an iron header bar that would have decapitated him if not for his rodeo skills. When he ducked under it at the last minute, I remember thinking, *Damn, he IS a cowboy.* He said he was and showed me a check for $150 with "cow punchy" written in the Memo that he saved in a scrapbook with other mementos of a life stranger than fiction – Ronnie's. A check from Warner Brothers for $200 gets an honorable mention. If you ask him, it's his silver-screen debut, not ½ a second of screen time as an extra in the Sean Connery "non-classic," *Just Cause.*

I've run class five rapids that others portaged around on the Deschutes River, climbed shear rock faces, repelled off two-hundred-foot ledges, and climbed the most technical peak in Oregon – Mt. Jefferson.

You haven't been cold until camped at ten thousand feet high in February in the Colorado Rockies. Snowshoeing to the top of the bowl, hoping not to need the avalanche training, we dropped in - carving deep swaths in the fresh powder until reaching the tree line. Separating the men from the boys, snowboarding the backcountry isn't for the faint of heart. Negotiating around deep tree wells at speed, voids that can end up your grave should you find yourself upside down in one, snow-packed in your mouth, nose, and ears. I speak from experience, as I'd be clothes with bones if not for this strapping young lad from Delaware who pulled me out of one.

Fast forward a couple of decades, and I stumble upon what some say is an ability to spin a yarn, and here we are. I am your ambassador to the outdoors, the Sportsman's consigliere representing our interests to the masses of uninformed and confused who think Southern outdoorsmen are ignorant to the environment's plight by default. May these stories provide clarity to those confused about the meaning of sportsmanship and how it relates to conservation.

From the mountains to the sea, I roam by whatever means necessary – technical poling skiff or little bateau (jon boat), foot or hoof, wheels or wings. A free-range outdoor nomad, I live for the experience. I must, because I lose more than I win, yet I keep showing up.

I keep taking risks, physical and legal, in search of adventure.

I have put in my 10,000 hours as a sportsman, and I'm here to tell you that if everyone would get outside, the world would be a better place. Mother Nature is gender-neutral and can't see color. Come one, come all, *laissez les bon temps rouler* (let the good times roll). I speak my mind, stand my ground, and stick up for the little guy. I wear flip-flops and a cowboy hat and run a backwater ghost named the *Honey Badger.* I am the Saltwater Cowboy.

—Jon Edward Edwards

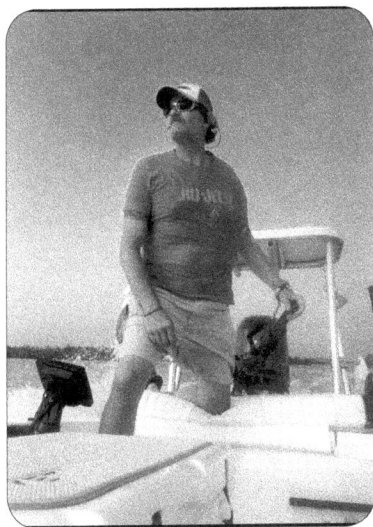

1

10,000 Islands Paradox

Riding better describes my skiff's modus operandi other than *driving* in that it takes a measure of coordination and trained sea legs to run it as it is meant to be run. Seventy horsepower doesn't seem like much in a world of four-hundreds, but it is a lot of power in your left palm, as my outboard is controlled by a handle – tiller style. Like rack and pinion in a Jag, it will turn on a dime but will also get away from you fast, which is what happened on that crisp early winter's day with a light and variable east wind and good water clarity.

      With the sun at my back cutting the glare, I could see clear around the crab pots. One stone crab buoy line after another, I weaved in and out, searching for the wayward tripletail floating about aimlessly, waiting for an easy meal.

I came to the end of one row and turned to catch the first buoy in the next row, but my hand slipped off the throttle. The torque pushed the motor to the right, and out I went. The brisk water and adrenaline dump were a sensory overload. It took a couple of seconds to process the event. I saw my boat … coasting, settling into its wake.

Thankfully, the killswitch was attached to a para-cord bracelet on my wrist. However, it was flapping like crazy in my breaststroke, significantly slowing my forward progress. I unclipped the bracelet, balled up the cord, shoved it in the pocket of my shorts, then sprinted for the skiff. Good for me, it was down current.

"Whew …" I thought, climbing aboard. *"That really got out of hand fast …"* When I dried off and my faculties returned, I realized my tripletail outing was not only a complete and total failure but a near disaster. *C'est la vie …* I turned inward towards the backcountry; maybe *the trout are biting.*

Once safely back in one of my prized honey-holes, I began trolling around making calculated casts at oyster and mangrove points, giving special attention to holes, troughs, and depressions. I presented the jig softly beyond a drop-off on the edge of a deep mangrove point and bounced it into the hole. *Bang!* He hit it like a Mack Truck, nearly jerking the rod out of my hand.

Nice redfish … I managed to get the trolling motor pointed away from the mangroves while maintaining a tight line between myself and the fish that was surging on the other end, peeling drag. We battled back and forth until I got him close enough to see that it wasn't a redfish. OK... *black drum*. Upon closer inspection, I realized it wasn't a black drum either but the biggest tripletail I'd ever caught.

It was slick calm as I glided across the bay into a setting sun. Red reflected off the water in the distance, where the last of the sun's rays cut through a break in the tall mangroves. In the fading light, I wondered how one goes from falling out of the boat running buoys for tripletail only to catch two (one a personal best) in the backcountry. *Easy*, it occurred to me – just spend enough time in the 10,000 Islands, where anything can, and will, happen.

2

Good Morning, Camper

Oh man ... great spot, I thought, looking around for the catch. There must be one, a pristine campsite like this all to myself? I ran the skiff up on the beach for further inspection. The strip was big enough for one camp only, had deep water on one side and a sandy shoal. *Shoot, this is it.*

After schlepping copious amounts of gear, of which I would use but a fraction, and setting up camp, I plopped down in my fancy folding chair pointing west towards a rapidly setting sun. I cracked a cold beer and said cheers to my companion, the Everglades.

An authoritative voice booming, "Good morning, camper," was not the greeting I expected on the first morning of my Inaugural Annual Spiritual Serenity Solo – or so I'm calling it. Dolphins crashing bait or just waves lapping softly against the beach is more along the lines of what I had in mind.

"Uhh … good morning," I replied.

"Sir, before you step out of the tent, I need to know if you have any weapons inside." Whoa, there went my serenity. Visions of standing in a federal courtroom after a third offense for running in a Slow Speed Manatee Zone flashed before my eyes. I vividly remember the judge peering at me over his glasses and saying, "Son, I better not see you in here again." My argument of how a West Indian Manatee knows where it is safe and where it isn't didn't go over very well. Thankfully, the judge was kind, or maybe he just appreciated quality humor, but he let me off light with a stiff fine, nonetheless. Since then, I've done my best to follow the rules - or so I thought.

"Yes sir, I do," I told him what I was packing while racking my brain, trying to figure out what prompted the visit from The Man in Green. Then I remembered I had forgotten to renew my registration. *That must be it ... whew*. I felt a little bit better as I crawled out of my tent; a custom model hastily made from parts and pieces of several defunct Walmart units, and faced my serenity bandits, as there were two officers. *Oh man - they must have run my background, seen the priors, and called in the Calvary!* Come to find out, I was giving myself way too much street cred, and the Game Wardens knew me not as the Manatee Bandit but more the moron who doesn't know he's in a restricted area.

"May I help you?" I asked them as if they had interrupted me during an important meeting.

Holding up his ticket book, the lead Game Warden said, "Well, Mr. Edwards, we've got seven issues here."

Seven!!! I nearly blurted out. *Oh lord, I'm going to prison.* But all that came out of my mouth was, "Seven? Huh …"

"Did you know this area is restricted to camping?"

"No sir, I did not. But that would explain why I had it all to myself." The comment earned a chuckle from both men. I asked for permission, then pulled up the Navionics app on my phone and showed them the big box over the key in which we stood that said **CAMPING AREA**. The officers looked at each other and said at the same time, "Yeah…" Officer #2 finished their thought, "That's wrong. We've been saying something should be done about it." There was an awkward pause as I waited for him to elaborate. Instead, he said, "You're also in the national park, which requires a permit and proof of the completion of a boater safety class. And you have neither."

The fact that I was in the Everglades National Park was news to me as I explained that I generally stay closer to the Goodland area where there are no such requirements. But due to favorable weather and calm seas, I had decided to venture further south or east, I might say. It hadn't occurred to me that I had slipped over into the national park. Officer #2 acted like he hadn't heard me when he said, "Sir, do you know your campfire has to be no farther than the high tide line? He motioned to the smoldering embers in a sandpit I dug a few feet from my tent.

"No sir, I did not," I replied, wondering how the fire was supposed to deter the No-see-um's - the die-hard hold-outs from summer - way down there by the water. I kept it to myself.

OK, that's four (camping in a restricted area, no permit, no boater's safety, and improper fire or something); three more to go. Expired registration, I knew about that one. No type 3 throwable … *Dangit!* The other violation seems to have slipped my mind for the moment. Out of the graciousness of the lead officer's heart, he only ticketed me for camping in a restricted area.

The moral of the story is that although the 10,000 Islands is wild and somewhat untamed, it is not an open range free-for-all. There may be permits to get, boater's safety classes to be taken, and of course, rules and regulations to follow. Those who know me well, go ahead and laugh it up, for I realize that statement coming from me is laughable. The scrapbook full of citations, including the summons for the federal charge, is a testament to the fact.

A coast guard helicopter buzzed me as I meandered my way back towards Goodland. My paranoia sharp and constant, my heart fluttered, and a pang of anxiety hit me. *What have I done now?*

I would like to clarify that although my stories are based primarily on actual events, there are individual artistic freedoms taken for one reason or another. I wasn't joking about the violations; that is all true. But my flippant attitude towards them is an attempt at humor, as is any disrespectful dialogue, as there was absolutely none. These are all serious matters, and I have nothing but the utmost respect for all law officers – on and off the water.

3

Coming in Hot

"Hang on! Coming in hot!" I yelled over the loudness of the antiquated twenty-five horse Yamaha two-stroke. Heading into a break-neck bend in a narrow backwater creek, the steering cable snapped. Skipping and sliding, we careened into the rubbery confines of mangrove. Branches slapping and spider webs draping, we finally came to a stop wedged in there good.

At the time, my skiff was a sixteen-foot flat-bottom aluminum hull controlled from the bow with a stick, not unlike an airboat. Custom welded casting deck, sixteen-gallon fuel tank, and bow-mounted trolling motor; it was a backcountry ghost. Which is appropriate, considering we disappeared into the mangrove system.

"You aight!" I hollered through a series of rapid spits, "*thpp, thpp, thpp,*" attempting to clear the cobweb from my mouth.

"I'm good!" Will, my eleven-year-old son (at the time), yelled from the rear.

After pulling ourselves out with fistfuls of mangrove branches, I began trolling out of the creek to a marked river where we could be rescued.

My dad had his flats boat at Caloosa Island Marina. There was still plenty of time left in the day for him to get from his house in Marco to the marina and reach our location before dark. I knew it was big ask for anyone. But since I'd once heard Dad exclaim, "I don't think I've ever NOT run aground," I gave him an out. "No big deal if you don't want to tackle it. I can call SeaTow. I need to get a membership anyway." I wasn't surprised nor bent out of shape when he took me up on it.

I wasn't off the phone with SeaTow five-minutes before he called back and told me to cancel SeaTow."

"Why?" I asked.

In a sharp tone, he said, "You'd come get me, wudn't ya?"

"Indeed, I would."

Anchored off a deep point adjacent to a massive oyster bar with steady outgoing water, Will was already hooked up. He slung the keeper-sized mangrove snapper into the boat, jaws steadily snapping, *bap, bap, bap.* As he popped the jig from its mouth, my son said something I'll never forget, "It's OK, Dad. It doesn't matter as long as we're together," oblivious to the gravitas of his statement.

With a soulful heart, I replied, "Exactly, Bubba … Exactly."

One hour went by with no communication. Consummate professionals, SeaTow, called back to ask if he had made it. I told them that he had not, and I wasn't able to reach him. But I couldn't leave if he was roaming around looking for us, not yet. I told SeaTow to stand by.

We caught more snapper as the sun sank over distant mangrove islands. Then the no-see-ums came out. Covering up in everything we could find, buffs, raincoats zipped all the way up, they still found a way in.

That's it, I called in the Cavalry.

Within forty-five minutes, SeaTow was there, had us hooked up, and we were on our way back to Goodland. Still no word from Dad.

As we turned the corner at Tripod Key, the sky lit up. Chopper canvasing - spotlight scanning, boats from the Sheriff's Department, Wildlife and Fisheries, and Fire Department. Coon Key Pass suddenly seemed small. Then, *BOOM,* the brightest light I'd ever seen trained on me. Over a bullhorn, I hear, "Jed Edwards?"

Having been no stranger to maritime violations, I threw my hands in the air and declared, "It wasn't me. My son and I have been broken down all afternoon!" I lowered my hands and relaxed a little when the bullhorn blared, "Your dad called 911."

Upon finally reaching him, Dad said, "Oh man… I ran the Honey Badger aground… my phone died… The tide came up a little – I made it to Coon Key Marina. Somebody was there and let me use the phone to call 911." The Honey Badger was Dad's twenty-six-foot center-console with twins that he kept docked at his house.

"What? I must say, the possibility that you would have attempted to bring the Honey Badger back there never occurred to me. Why didn't you just call SeaTow?"

"Hell, I don't know! I'd just been on a Chinese fire drill … I figured y'all would be about dead from inhaling no-see-ums by then. Hey, it would have been more bizarre if I HADN'T run aground." That earned a hearty laugh.

It's not about the win or the loss, or the kill or the catch – it's not about the trophy. That is all ancillary. It's about screaming drags and high fives, the thrill of the hunt, respect for mother nature, love of the outdoors, and a passion for wildlife. Cliché as it may be, my son and I are best friends. I believe that is directly related to the bonds forged during times like these, quests for adventure. Many people fail to understand that or are too ignorant to comprehend. Myself, I try not to speak to things of which I have no understanding.

4

How Many Wraps

The sun was high in the Southwest Florida sky on a balmy summer day off Marco Island, Florida. A slight Southwest wind blew across the Gulf of Mexico from the Yucatan Peninsula, absorbing the heat of the Gulf Stream along the way.

The water on the western side of Marco Island was a clear and vibrant turquoise with patches of green from the seagrasses mixed in. The towering condominiums of Caxambas Pass were visible above the tall mangroves that line Cape Romano.

A flock of brown pelicans glided gracefully, slowing to divebomb schools of bait. With reckless abandon, they hit the water with a force that would seemingly rip them apart. Tough birds they were – my favorite bird. They remind me of Cadillac Allante's.

The tide had been rushing in, swirling around the jagged metal piles of the Cape Romano Dome Houses. Making calculated drifts, we floated live greenback shiners past the structure.

"There he is," Ben, my customer and lifelong friend from North Louisiana, uttered as his hips thrust forward, his arms bowed, pulling against the creature surging on the other end. Rod bent nearly all the way over, the drag buzzed in spasms - *zzz... zzz... zzz...* as line was stripped from the reel. Music to my ears was the *high pitch whine* of the braided line as it was being reeled back through the guides of the rod.

A wide bucket mouth burst through the water from just outside the corner piling of the last Dome House. Followed by an expanse of silver and black sinew, the snook danced across the surface. All of a sudden … *Pop!* Ben and I exchanged a look – that look of mutual disbelief. Then, from the aft deck came a volley of obscenities. His fish was gone.

Ben reeled in the line - sure enough - a little squiggly. A tell-tale sign of a compromised knot – solidifying operator error. Those of you among the community of avid to expert light tackle anglers along the Gulf Rim understand …

"How many wraps did you use on that loop knot?" I asked, already aware that his answer, if honest, would be less than it should have been.

"Just one, same as always. Usually, it's not a problem." Ben was still looking at the "little squiggly" in disgust.

"It's got to be three wraps on the loop knot, man – not two, not three … maybe even four. One may be enough for those three-pound bass in North Louisiana, but not for a big snook. "That was the last greenback, Amigo," I said, pulling on a long cord, lifting the trolling motor out of the water. It folded down nicely; the pin "clicked" as it snapped into the base.

The boat was drifting dangerously close to the jagged and rusty metal beams of the Dome House. I hurried down the gunnel and plopped down on the bench seat. Without a moment to spare, I cranked the motor and punched the throttle. The little skiff danced across the still water, heading due north towards Caxambas Pass.

5

When You Can

I banked into the last turn of the narrow backwater creek a little bit too hot. Turning hard to port, the flat-bottomed aluminum boat nearly skipped into the mangroves. Quickly I backed off the throttle, regained control, then accelerated into the rest of the turn. From the slender creek I was spit out into an open expansive familiar bay, one in between Goodland and Chokoloskee.

Upon reaching my spot, I spun the boat one hundred and eighty degrees and idled back into an incoming tide inundated with bait. I shut down the engine and gently laid the anchor over the bow so as not to make any noise. Yet, I forgot to take into account the ten-foot length of chain attached to it. "Dddddddddd," rattling and clanging all the way down it went. Two roseate spoon-bills were spooked out of a cluster of deadwood. *Unbe-lievable.*

The wind had been blowing out of the west for days, churning up the Gulf and making a mess out of the backcountry, limiting my choices of spots to try. But here I was – this was a time *when I could fish*. Little did I know that I was on the cusp of the greatest sixty minutes of backwater angling of my life.

I played out enough anchor line so that I was po-sitioned just a cast away from the edge of two troughs that converged at an unassuming mangrove point. I could feel the braided line spin under a light thumb as I fired the foul smelling, one-quarter-ounce jig head complete with a soft plastic shad imitation, dark in color, towards the point. The jig fell into the trough, and I gave it a couple of bounces. *BOUNCE, BOUNCE. STOP.* Instinc-tively, I gave the rod a swift jerk only to have embedded it into a pile of oyster shells. *Dang it! Not first cast...* I grabbed the line directly in front of the reel with my left hand and pulled out about half an arm's length until it was fairly taut but not so much as to dig the hook any deeper. Quickly letting go of the line I snapped it back down. *Snap, snap, snap.* I repeated the process until the reverberation traveled through the long expanse of fluo-rocarbon leader and all the way to the hook, pushing out the other side.

One jig hop away from the averted set-back and, "Pow!" Something hit it with intent to inflict grievous bodily harm - no half measures; it was violent. A wide bucket mouth bust through the surface followed by an expanse of silver and black sinew that danced across the water. I rolled my wrists over and turned the big snook's head back down, lessening the chances of having a hook thrown. For several minutes we fought until I horsed the big Soap Fish along the side of the boat, popped the lure out of its rough mouth, and watched it swim off.

The bite was fast and furious for the better part of the next sixty minutes. The snook were biting, the trout were biting, the redfish were biting; everything was biting. I'm not sure how many fish, or species of fish, I ended up catching during that window of time. Had the conditions not been what they were would I have ended up there at the time that I was? Probably not. Would the comedy of errors that I had been "blessed" with normally have resulted in not getting a bite? Most likely.

As dusk drew near and I prepared the skiff for flight, something my grandfather told me came to mind. An adage that now carried a certain gravitas. When asked when was the best time to go fishing he replied, "When you can."

6

Debunked Banana

Picturesque South Florida spring day it was, two to three feet seas, clear skies, and clean water, anchored near an artificial reef five miles off the Naples coast - Capt. Joel Pepper was doing what he does – putting people on gamefish.

Five miles is hardly offshore, not to mention the vastness between there and the Gulf Stream. Yet there they were, hooked up to a pelagic species generally associated with blue-water and the Atlantic Ocean.

"What chu got there, Bud," Capt. Pepper says while videoing the angler/fish dance around the boat with

"Sailfish," the junior angler replied, his father cheering in the background.

"Oh no, we've already got one on the deck!" yelled Capt. Pepper, aiming the camera at the one-hundred-pound billfish lying on the bottom of the boat.

Sailfish? Near shore of Naples? Hogwash ... one might say. But nothing is outside the wheelhouse for Joel, averaging one or two sailfish hookups per season.

"Watch your fish; be careful," said Capt. Pepper to his charge. The young man shuffled from the stern up the bow and around, having found a rhythm with his opponent.

"That's a fish of a lifetime, son. People go all the way to Costa Rica to catch a fish like that. You just caught it." The angler turned the battle-fatigued fish one more time and brought it along the side of the boat. Deciding one sailfish was enough – even though they would have been well within regulation – Capt. Pepper reached over the side and removed the hook, making a clean release.

"Everybody says bananas on a boat are bad luck," Joel says into the video, holding a banana in front of the camera. "Here on my boat, in the Gulf of Mexico, we just caught a sailfish, actually caught two."

Not only was his catch phenomenal, but Capt. Pepper will go down in history as the waterman who debunked the banana on board superstition. I will thank Joel personally for freeing me of the 'banana chains" that have bound me. (Although fishermen are a superstitious lot, and I'm sure I'll just substitute another one in its place.)

I must say I have made considerable efforts keeping bananas out of my boat. Sometimes I go so far as to recite a generic pre-trip spiel, not unlike a flight attendant announcing that all cell phones must be turned off and tray tables put in the upright position.

The spiel would usually go something like this: "Before we embark on our journey, is anyone in possession of a banana, or bananas? If so, please deposit them in the waste can or toss them to that assertive pelican over there,"

I'm kidding about feeding fruit to pelicans. I generally don't give them anything but large filleted carcasses. I'm just playing; they have a proclivity for going big – as long as it almost fits in their mouth, which I imagine gives them a hell of a case of heartburn. Because I respect any creature whose heart is bigger than its brain, I make an effort not to endanger them.

For those outside the fishing community who are no doubt confused, feel free to google the origin of the banana superstition. Or maybe you could wait and see what The Saltwater Cowboy gets into next … A sci-fi thriller perhaps where he slips through a tear in the space-time continuum, landing in the 1700s when pirates, buccaneers, bandits, and marauders ruled the seas? When the fruit would sometimes spoil on the long trips from afar. Legend has it that a parasite found in the bananas was particularly fond of the hardwood the ships were made of, boring in, eventually eating enough to render the craft structurally unsound and subsequently sinking.

And now you know … the rest of the story.

That sounds more like a novel. Maybe a sequel to the future NY Times Bestseller, *Gulf Stream* by Jon Edward Edwards? I should probably focus on finding a publisher for the future bestseller first.

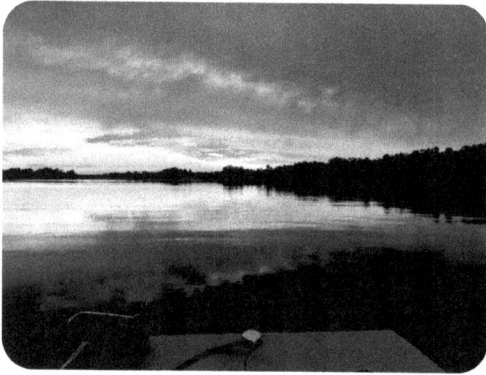

7

Purple Fade

Dusk brought a slight Southwest wind, dry and fresh. Magic Hour, one hour before sunset – my favorite time to fish. Thru the fancy Bluetooth earbuds that I paid way too much for came the lyric: *Out on the road today I saw a dead head sticker on a Cadillac*

The mangrove island in front of me was tall enough to block all signs of development, creating an illusion of wilderness. Making calculated casts with a lead jig-head complete with a soft-plastic offering, I trolled along, letting the jig sink all the way before retrieving. *Sink... (wait until the line goes slack), twitch... sink..., twitch.* The key is to retrieve line during the bounce, providing a perpetual motion with zero slack, giving the lure realism.

A big center console with twin screws (propellors) came by at a good clip. As it pushed its own wake, it scooped up bottoms of twilight, mixing bits of red into a purple fade on the Big Marco River. Pin-drip quiet in the anticipation of the strike - t*witch… sink… twitch.*

A little voice inside my head said don't go back, you can never go back...

8

Hoot Owl

Is this really happening, I wonder as the series of surreal events unfolded around me. From an airboat in a canal, deep within the Florida Everglades on the Miccosukee Indian Reservation, I watched Ronnie's airboat turn upside down and sink – in about the amount of time that it took to write this sentence. Jolted from my trance-like state by the alarm in his voice, I came around to the here and now. "Get over here!" Ronnie, my dad, yelled as he and his passengers dog-paddled in the alligator-infested waterway.

A marvelous morning of largemouth bass angling it had been. Tossing and flipping mostly watermelon-colored soft plastic baits threaded on weedless hooks, we ripped lip after lip … a saving grace after the previous night's series of surreal events left the trip in jeopardy of becoming a complete bust. Yet, at this point, the saving grace morphed into a diabolical and potentially Major League Baseball career-ending disaster.

Our guests at The Hoot Owl that weekend were members of the Texas Rangers Baseball Organization. At that time, the Ranger's spring training facility was in Port Charlotte, and a life-long friend of mine, Ken Guthrie, happened to be the bullpen catcher.

An interesting anecdote is that Ken had made headline sports news during the prior baseball season; albeit news doused in controversy. As a joke among friends, Ken had thrown a ball to outfielder Rusty Greer in which he had written a profanity-laden message. This message included a term that may or may not have had certain racial undertones – "redneck." It depends on who you're asking. Those of us from the Deep South consider it a term of endearment. Rusty immediately began throwing the ball around the outfield without noticing said message. When the inning started, Juan Gonzales (another outfielder), unaware of the harmlessly intended sentiment, flipped the ball to an awaiting fan. The fan turned the ball into the San Diego Padres officials, claiming the message was intended for him or her - I can't remember which. Which was odd considering the term was one particularly associated with southern white males, of which the fan was not. Ken was forced to explain the story and was lightly reprimanded. The rest is history.

The weekend started interestingly enough with two madmen in fan boats wearing spelunker helmets outfitted with one-million candlepower headlamps racing through the Everglades approaching the boat landing. The two madmen being Ronnie, and his partner in the Hoot Owl camp, George Smith, R.I.P.

Another fact worth mentioning is that George invented the willow-leaf spinner bait, according to Roland Martin in a 1969 edition of Bass Master Magazine. Also, I would be amiss not to mention that George taught me much of what I know about the 10,000 Islands.

Myself, Ken, an All Star starting (left-handed) pitcher, a short stop, and the bullpen coach loaded onto the two airboats and sped into the dark of night toward the famed Hoot Owl camp. Those who loaded onto Ronnie's "sled", as the type of airboats are called that are designed to slide through the sawgrass, had unwillingly just reduced their life expectancy significantly. Not that Ronnie is a poor operator. On the contrary, his exceptional skills were the only reason there had been no loss of life.

Turning into an indistinguishable break in the foliage, we came to a narrow path overgrown with vines and limbs blocked by a chain that spanned from two cypress trees. Killing the engine, Ronnie stepped down and unhooked the chain. In a tree to his right was a stop sign that had to be as old as we were – an oddity in the midst of the swamp. Grabbing handfuls of branches, we pulled ourselves into the centuries old cypress hammock that opened into a shallow lagoon. In the center of the lagoon was the two-story behemoth of a camp built out of pressure-treated lumber on pilings, all material being brought in little by little via airboat. Not your typical camp, the Hoot Owl had all the comforts of a reasonably modern home.

Excited was the only way to describe the vibe, which intensified when Ronnie asked if anyone wanted to go gator hunting. As the baseball players loaded onto Ronnie's airboat, Ken and mine's protests were drowned out over the deafening noise. We looked at each other as if to say, "This isn't going to be good for anybody."

Several anxiety laden hours later, the crew came limping (literally and figuratively) back to the camp. The mood was now somber as the pitcher was holding his el-bow – the left one. Whether or not they were successful in their gator hunt, I can't say … as such activities were forbidden on the reservation. However, what I can say is that Ronnie had hit a cypress knee, throwing the pitcher into the front of the airboat.

The next morning everyone was fine, including the pitcher, who seemed to have made it unscathed – pitching arm intact. We all breathed sighs of relief as we loaded up into the airboats and headed for the canal to fish. Unbeknownst to us, the encounter with the cypress knee had punctured a hole in Ronnie's airboat, which we couldn't see due to the airboat's surface being entirely decked over. And thus ensued the horror of seeing the aforementioned airboat flip upside down, sink, and professional baseball players swim in a canal crawling with gators.

I don't remember hearing much about the pitcher after that. I can only hope it wasn't because of our little adventure. But as we rode through the Everglades taking the crew back to the boat landing, I remember thinking, *This is going to make one hell of a story.*

9

Looking a Little Green

As a student of the fishing game and an all-around out-door enthusiast, I'll jump at any opportunity for adventure, on and off the high seas. If there's one arena in which I lack professional class experience, it's offshore. So, when one of the top offshore guides in the area asked me to First Mate on a red snapper trip, I felt like I'd been called up to the majors.

I showed up at the customers' place on Marco Island, ready to rock and roll, fancy pliers clipped to my belt and all. The owners of the 35′ Boston Whaler were a group of friends from Chicago. A rowdy bunch, not unlike us, just with a weird accent. (Those who know me will appreciate the irony of that statement – me referencing an accent.) These guys had come to fish, ready to rumble, expecting a meat haul. We headed out of Big Marco Pass and hammered down, the rising sun at our backs.

Several miles out, one of the guys started to look a little green. I leaned over and yelled over the noise of the engines, "Hey, Podna. You alright? Lookin' a little green there. Did you take any Dramamine?" He said he hadn't. One of the other guys broke some out of his bag and gave it to him. I gave a little spiel on sea-sickness; keep your eye on the horizon, stay hydrated … like I was a seasoned veteran. Shortly afterward, Mr. Green seemed fine.

Eighty miles offshore in 165 feet of water, the Captain found the snapper, and they were ravenous; big ones too. Running from the back of the boat to the front, side to side, taking them off hooks, measuring them, and either boxing or letting them go. Grouper were mixed in as well, and cobia showed up as I cut squid and herring, baited hooks, and tied snapped leaders.

Suddenly I began to feel a little puny. I tried to push through, but it got worse. My body ceased to work. I got worried, unaware of what was happening to me. *Dehydration, kidney stones?* I told the Captain, "Hey, Amigo. Something is amiss. If my face starts drooping, or I start slurring my words, call in a mayday, or a pan-pan … something. Because I might be having a stroke."

Then, the gentleman I had lectured regarding the ins and out of seasickness said, "Hey, are you alright? Looking a little green there." *OMG,* I thought. *I'm sea-sick…*

I had been seasick once in my life, Cabo San Lucas, in the year of our Lord nineteen hundred and ninety-eight. The former Mrs. Edwards and I were on our honeymoon, bill fishing. It's the only time I've ever caught marlin. Although, I couldn't enjoy much of it because I was sick as a dog. However, I think that was due more to the spirits the night before. Or it could have been the Mexican Xanax. And my divorce came as a shock …

This was different. In addition to the spectacular vomit volleys, the fatigue and nausea were crippling. Although, the worst, by far, was the embarrassment. I'd blown my Big League debut. Not only could I not do my job, but now I had to be seen after.

In the name of self-preservation, I must say that I rallied a few hours later, somewhat saving face. Thankfully, the Captain is a dear friend and waited until after the charter to tell me what a jackass I am.

Since then, I take a Dramamine before going offshore and no longer give advice on seasickness.

It seems as if I have more epic fails than cosmic wins. But I'd rather shoot for the moon and miss than aim for the ditch and make it.

10

Spring Tide Rock Pile

Since the late 2000s, post-financial challenges when I afforded an offshore worthy vessel, I find myself reminiscing about my beloved Rock Pile every summer spring
tide. I visualize being at the helm of my 26' Edgewater,
eating up the seas, slicing and deflecting any spray that
may have otherwise sandblasted the facial region. Legs
bending with the rhythm of the waves, feeling the water
beneath me, timing them, it was an exercise in serenity.

     Many times – offshore in general - the peace and
serenity are replaced by fear and anxiety, for Florida Bay
can become treacherous without any warning. Any of
my saltwater brethren who have become intimate with
lightning know what I mean. One must pay attention,

watch for the omens, and be prepared to call the dogs and pee on the fire.

Ignorance and a lack of respect for Mother Nature is an excellent way to find yourself searching for floating flotsam and praying the Coast Guard beats hypothermia. Having confidence in yourself as a captain and in your vessel is imperative; water coordination – sea legs – mandatory.

The Rock Pile, a site unknown to other saltwater anglers, is sacred to me and a select few trusted fishing compadres. The GPS numbers - I'll suffer torturous acts and not divulge - reeds under the fingernails, public floggings with ten-foot bamboo shafts – none the matter.

The coordinates were shared in confidence by an accomplished offshore guide and dear friend, Captain Glenn Andrews. Glenn was a champion, and the world is a little bit dimmer without him in it, like a fluorescent bulb that doesn't entirely burn as bright as it once did. Rest in peace, my friend.

My crew and I (they will remain nameless) would arrive at the Rock Pile a few hours before dusk, giving us just enough time to get set up before a time I call "Magic Hour." The residents of this South Florida luxury water condominium consist mainly of the upper class. The most prominent being clan snook. Some other high-society types being snapper, grouper, cobia, and permit.

During the summer months, many of the big Labradors (snook – look at them between the eyes, and you'll see it) have either moved offshore to spawn or have spawned. The fertile Rock Pile is like a giant maternity ward for big sow snook and the smaller yet strapping males circling, protecting the hatch.

Of course, this time of year is catch and re-lease and release only. Anyone kind enough to follow the Saltwater Cowboy knows my propensity for opposing authority. It must be the 80's skateboarder in me. Rule-bending ways aside, I am a sportsman. Thus, by default, a conservationist.

Blessed be the anonymous and remarkable individual, or individuals, who created the reef. I would like to clarify that the individual was not myself. A permit is required from the state and approved by the USCG for artificial reefs.

The Rock Pile does have a dark side, having been taken over in a hostile manner by the greedy and gluttonous Goliath Grouper. They are the big kid that smacks you in the back of the head and takes your lunch money. As anglers, they aggravate us due to their larcenous ways and cheap shots. They are grossly unsportsmanlike; they wait and take advantage by rushing out from their rocky lair and eating the disabled captive - sometimes leaving the head as some kind of sick joke. Occasionally they will let go. I've seen snook brought in deader than a doornail, mangled and slimy from being crushed by those massive jowls.

At one time, an endangered species, a moratorium was placed on them, making it illegal to take one of any size. The Goliath made for an easy target due to their size and lackadaisical attitude. A spearfisherman could swim right up to one, and "Bang!" Although, this is usually not a good idea considering some of them are the size of Volkswagens and could take a diver on a tremendous ride. However, in my opinion, recreational fishing and spearfishing took a small percentage of the blame for their decline. Some say they have made a complete recovery as they are plentiful in this region of the Gulf.

A jig fisherman, me, I would bounce a heavy two-to-three-ounce jig head with a soft plastic around the edges of the pile. That's where the big snook liked to loiter. The trick is to bounce the line but time the retrieve evenly, so as not to get any slack. *Bounce... bounce... bounce...*

The curiousness of a cobia is their Achilles heel, cruising along, eager to accept a flipped pinfish or other lively bait. A notorious screamer of reel drags, permit would make frequent appearances and are addicted to small blue crabs. Of course, many were lost to the Goliath. Once the sun dipped, the snapper bite would turn on.

After the bait was gone and the crew tired from wrangling, we secured the gear and ensured the catch was iced. Lastly, I engaged the electric windlass, pulled the anchor from the Rock Pile, pointed the bow due north, and navigated home in the dark – my beloved Rock Pile in the rear view – its anonymity preserved.

11

Ride the Lightning

On a picturesque 10,000 Islands summer day drifting with the incoming tide along the Fakahatchee River, the tarpon were rolling almost on top of one another. They weren't the big bruisers that the record chasers followed from Homosassa to Islamorada for decades. Tom Evans, Steve Huff, and Thomas McGuane come to mind. These fish, dark from the tannic backwater, were around the forty to sixty-pound class.

My compadre, Hegar, and I had never seen tarpon so eager to inhale a bait. Therefore, as sportsmen, we made a conscious decision to ignore the incoming weather system. Comfortably numb to the danger among the zinging drags and snapped leaders, a thermocline settled in, and the temperature dropped. The taste in the air reminded me of when a friend dared me to lick a 9-volt battery, which I did. Thunder began to crack. The western horizon was a sinister black with streaks of grey, shards of lightning spiking at close intervals.

But the greenback shiner on the end of my line was looking sexy with his #5 circle hook nose ring. I'd lobbed the bait up current, leaving enough slack for the live pilchard to make his way to an eddy between two mangrove lay-downs. I stood at the bow, hip against the trolling motor handle, making slight adjustments to the boat position. Unlike the aggressive strike from most gamefish of the region, a more appropriate description of a tarpon bite is to subtly abscond with unmatched speed and agility. Tense as one of those goats that faint upon varying degrees of stress, hand white-knuckled around the Calcutta 400, the water erupted around my bait. *Gulp! Zzzzzzzzzz ...Another fish on!*

"Man, this isn't looking good," Hegar said as I pulled hard to the inside, trying to turn the fish's head and stop its blistering run before I was out of line.

"Aww, it's just a clear up shower," I replied as the bottom fell out of the sky.

"Clear up shower?" Hegar said, wondering if he'd heard me right.

"Yeah, clear up to your ass." Our fear became all too real as the lightning strikes were no longer distant, but close, real close. We scrambled, taking the rods out of the holders and laying them down on the deck. Careless we were, but not dumb enough to surround ourselves with lightning rods. We jammed the boat as far as we could into the mangrove foliage and hunkered down. I might have even recited a little prayer under my breath.

About thirty sphincter clinching minutes later the electrical storm moved to the SSW, but another system was looming behind it. If we're going to get the hell out of Dodge now was the time.

Pushing the Pathfinder to its limit southbound on the serpentine tidal river the rain felt like shards of fiberglass pelting your bare skin, stinging like a tattoo machine, *bzzzzzzzzz* - relentless and unforgiving. In almost zero visibility I realized how well I knew my backwater path as I felt my way across Faka Union Bay, through Panther Key, and behind Four Brothers Key. Crossing Dismal Key Pass I looked south over the Gulf. Squinting through the rain, I saw a lightning bolt as thick as an old live oak tree spike from a thunderhead and grow four jagged legs, like a demonic Eiffel Tower dancing across the water.

We finally made it to the Goodland Bridge, rode hard and pruned from the relentless deluge. Idling into, what was in 2002, Moran's Barge Marina the world erupted in a white flash. The whitest of all whites.

In junior high school in Monroe, Louisiana, one of my chores was cutting the grass with my Dad's Yazoo push mower, the kind with large diameter Skyway Mag wheels, yellow in color. Imagine pushing a pallet jack loaded with drywall, but a little bit lighter. One day the engine began shaking and shimmying uncontrollably. I thought something looked loose, the sparkplug maybe. In my infinite wisdom, with the motor running, I decided to grab it. My hand fused to the engine block and my arm felt as if a Russian Slap Champion wielding a cattle prod shook the hell out of it. That's the sensation I felt when the residual electricity crawled up the throttle into my right arm.

Hegar and I lifted ourselves off the bottom of the boat where we had atavistically retreated upon the event. The lightning strike was so close that it took us a few seconds to determine whether or not we were still of this world. Hegar looked his arms up and down, felt around on his legs and body, mouth agape. I held my hand in front of my face expecting to find it filleted with burn exits. We looked at each other in disbelief. We were fine.

I'm sure we looked like trauma victims as we tied up to the dock, having been meters away from riding the lightning on a direct train to electrocution. It was then I reckoned it might behoove me to pay more attention to thunderstorms building in the Gulf of Mexico.

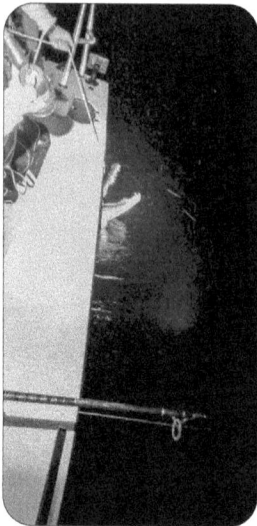

12

Beavertail Sandwich

The sun was low on the horizon as we sliced down the Upper Caloosahatchee Waterway in my 17' Beavertail Skiff. When we came around a bend facing due west, the reflection of the sunbeam off the water looked like a barrel of fire. I lined my eye up with the bright orange sight at the end. Barren and pastoral, mangrove shores on both sides, silver water, still in the near dusk hour. No one said a word. The bow hopped, bouncing wind off the slick water, popping my ears. The four of us focused like a team of Tier One Special Forces Operators.

That may be stretching it a bit, and I'm not trying to steal any valor. However, we did have two gator tags to fill, which qualifies as a Special Operation - with a dangerous and formidable opponent. We *were* a team; everyone had a position.

When the sun had set, and darkness fell, we trolled the banks, scanning with powerful headlamps and flashlights, searching for pairs of eyes – red eyes. Coop and I stood on the bow, slapping at mosquitoes; me on the trolling motor holding a light, and Coop holding a stout grouper rod with a 12/0 treble hook and a 2-ounce lead weight.

"Arrigader, one o'clock," I said, taking a knee. Operating the trolling motor in my left hand, I held the flashlight steady on the red dots with my right. Coop fired a cast over my head like a catcher throwing to second base, but beyond, launching the grappling system well beyond the alligator.

"What did you say?" Bill Murray asked with a laugh. We call Coop's dad Bill Murray due to the slight resemblance. I can kind of see it, but mostly it's just fun to call him that. Although, one such as I must be careful, as this Bill Murray is a former professional hockey player who keeps himself in shape. As such, he could pound me into the ground like a two-pound sledgehammer on a stake. He's kind of like a coach, but a cool one. Not the one that walked the sidelines with a chinstrap, just looking for a reason to wrap someone on the helmet with the button end …, *BING!*

"That's how they say alligator over there in the backwoods of the Mississippi River Delta," Coop said to his dad as he reeled like a madman until the treble hook was just beyond the prehistoric beast.

"Yeah," I made a half turn to Bill Murray and repeated, "Arrigader." He just shook his head. Coop pulled the tackle into the gator with a fast-sweeping motion of the rod, to which it took offense. The hook never hit home, and the angry gator sulked away.

We continued the hunt as I poured sweat, moving from cove to cove, canal to canal, looking for The Big One, humidity so thick you could cut it with a hatchet.

Stopping in the middle of a large reservoir off the river packed with lily pads, Coop brought out the blue tooth speaker and synced it with his phone. Through the speaker came a series of chirping croaks, the sound made by juvenile alligators; the equivalent to a hail call at a flock of mallards high in a bluebird sky, eyeballing a decoy spread in a flooded rice field. It didn't take long before Ashley spotted a set of eyes the size of Red Delicious apples making way towards us.

I ducked down and held my light on the set of eyes. Coop catapulted the medieval-looking contraption well beyond the alligator. *Reelreelreelreel ...,* he closed the distance, but the gator darted forward. I followed him with the light. Coop adjusted course with the rod until the egg sinker was directly behind him. Then, *Wham!* Coop set the hook, and we began to have ourselves a rodeo.

The gator took off towards the river. Big... real big - we guessed about twelve feet. I chased it out of the lake and into the main river, Coop keeping steady pressure, gaining line as he could. A long and arduous battle ensued, and Coop nearly had the gator whipped. I was now using the trolling motor in closer quarters, making strategic moves in tandem with the direction of the fight.

Ashely, Coop's girlfriend, an accomplished outdoors-woman in her own right, held the light while I kept us in position. It turns out that professional hockey players from Canada have Cowboy skills because Bill Murray lassoed the gator like a team roper.

Then, in an instant, the trolling motor stopped. "What happened!" hollered Coop, changing direction, tugging the giant head in the opposite direction, away from the bank.

I lifted the trolling motor out of the water and turned the handle. The prop spun but barely. "Snapped cotter pin!" I yelled back. The gator had pulled us dangerously close to a steep bank, jagged with rip-rap.

By the time I ran down the gunnel and fired the engine, the gator had twisted tight to the boat and was having a sandwich of the port bow. I can still hear the teeth grinding the fiberglass, *Crunch, Crunch, Crunch* ... Just like that, repeatedly. "Hey, Man!" I shouted as if someone sprayed sunscreen all over my cushions. I got the motor going and backed us away from the bank. Bill Murray held fast, but the gator swung its head 180 degrees to the other side and chomped at it. "Hey! You're running up a bill here, Man!"

Big Boy got caught in the chewed-up rub rail alongside the boat, getting the rope in a bind, pulling the hook free. The Leviathan swam away free to do as they do – survive.

My battle injured Beavertail brought us back to the boat ramp, beaten but breathing, innards displayed and all. Fortunately, Coop and Bill Murray are competent at fiberglass work.

All in the name of adventure. If you're going to be a bear, be a grizzly.

13

White Pelicans

She had olive-toned skin; hair sun-kissed at the ends. She could have been a professional tennis player. Maybe she was … It's not like he'd never seen famous people in the Havana Cafe.

He thought of her as he followed the wind trail across the shoal. *I can see you, brown skin shining in the sun…*

A flock of white pelicans loitered on the lee side of a familiar key as he banked into a grassy depression and shut the engine down. He walked the wake down to the bow and engaged the trolling motor; old school style – no GPS control.

The day was beautiful and reminded him of the '90s when the grass was healthier, the trout bigger, and the area less traveled.

He didn't know what about her had him thinking in lyrics, *you got the top pulled back, and the radio up, baby* ... Her devilishly good looks or what she said, with emerald green eyes, in accented English, "I had to come all the way to Florida to find freedom."

As he meandered through the outer Pavilion Keys, he imagined how it must've looked back in the days of the outlaw Edgar Watson and Everglades City lore, and realized it was the latter.

Homeward bound in fading light her statement was put in perspective. *It doesn't get any freer than this...*

14

Hold on Loosely

He told her to hang on and opened the throttle all the way up. The skiff shot out of the water like a bat out of hell. Seventy horses in his left palm accessible with a twist of a tiller handle. Her tan leg flexed as she braced it against the side of the boat, hand cupped under the gunnel, rolling with the rhythm like it wasn't her first rodeo. He surfed across a quartering Coon Key Pass to Sugar Bay, twisting, skipping, and hitting straight a-ways all the way to the Blackwater River.

There was a nice oyster bar tucked in a flat off a river main point that he needed to try. He stopped up-current, cut the motor, snatched a live shrimp the size of a prawn from the live well, and pushed a circle hook under the horn in front of the black spot. It dangled two feet under a popping cork with every bit of one once.

She made a ninety-degree turn with her body, loaded the tip, and made a swooping cast. The line rolled off the spool, bumping her finger-tip until about two o'clock when she caught it in the first crease and flipped the bail on the spinning reel. Not only did she not sling the bait off, but she dropped in the strike zone. This was nothing to sneeze at.

They drifted. Big Boy got nervous, jumping out of the water like a scalded dog. The cork disappeared. "You gonna get that?" He snickered, watching the line move away.

Distracted by a flock of curlews loitering in the mangroves, the rod was nearly snatched from her hands. *"Zzzzz, Zzzzz, Zzzzz …,"* the drag zinged, and she felt the weight and strength of the fish as it swam against the incoming water, the rod bending in surges.

"Oh Oh …" he said with quick breaths, "You got a big ole good un." He got out of her way and took the Boga Grip out of the rear console. She fought the over-slot-sized redfish alongside the boat where I closed the Boga around its lip and lifted it out of the water. After a quick photo, he laid the fish back in the water, moved it around a little bit, and released it to watch it swim away.

Negotiating the snap bends of Gill Rattle Creek with quick bursts of acceleration, losing control then gaining it back, and trimming it out on the straight-a-ways, he chose all the right turns to Buttonwood Bay. They caught trout, snapper, ladyfish, and one too many hardhead catfish moving from point to point. With their poisonous fins, sliming the line … One flip away from a life of pain, you are (for the next however long.)

As he walked down the narrow gunnel to leave, a manatee surfaced and gave the boat a playful bump, near-ly sending him overboard. She laughed hard and made a futile attempt to video an act of nature in its purist form that few rarely see. She didn't need to record it. How can the memory be made viewed through a lens? With a flip of its massive fantail, it waved goodbye, the white flesh around three propeller scars on its back waned into But-tonwood Bay's muddy water.

He navigated hazards by memory east across the bay to a narrow cut that led to the mouth of another tight and serpentine creek. After a quick stop at a mangrove snapper hole, he ran across Dismal Key Pass, behind White Horse Key, and past what used to be the grass flats of Hog Key onto Panther Key.

They walked along the beach at Panther, stepping that way you do barefoot over shells, like on hot coals that aren't hot. Whitebait darted in and out of sandy de-pressions, silver flashes fading to deeper water. Her legs were "all day" long, and he admired her physique in the

bikini as she walked ahead, seemingly not as tender foot-
ed as he.

Eyes the color of the water beneath the Sev-
en-Mile Bridge in the Keys, she was the kind that rel-
egated him to brunettes and the occasional redhead. Allergic to blondes, he was, breaking out in broken hearts.
What hell it must be to be allergic to your addiction.

An East wind knocked down the seas for the ride
from Panther to Cape Romano. Gullivan Bay was turquoise clear, and he easily stayed in the troughs around
the sand bars. Their view of The Cape Romano Dome
Houses looked far offshore when they rounded the Cape,
like something out of a science fiction novel.

He knew of a tiny river tucked behind a wide
sand bar that only boats like his could access. From within, the view of the Gulf was unobstructed, but from the
Gulf looking in, it was secluded. Several yards off the
beach, he shoved a long pole into the sand and tied the
boat to it so they wouldn't be aground when the tide fell.

They got out in knee-deep water and waded to
the shoreline where the beach ended and swam to the

center of the river. The current whisked them back towards the boat while jacks busted, snapper popped, and, in the distance, the violent sound of a snook destroying something rang out ... *BLEOW!*

As the end of the day drew near, they sat on the poling platform drinking Shiner Bock. The western sky was pink streaked against towering thunderheads, and rain fell in grey sheets to the north. The setting sun was the only measure of time. It was as if they were the only people on the planet.

15

Knife to a Gun Fight

In the pre-dawn blackness of an overcast morning, we ran the Manatee River towards Tampa Bay. Crossing the bay, I could see the lights of the Sunshine Skyway Bridge over my right shoulder disappear into the clouds. The bruised sky of daylight coming up at our backs, Shannon pointed the bow north-northwest and engaged the autopilot. Outward Bound once again

The seas were calm enough for the teenagers (Shannon's daughter, Sydney, and my son, Will) to plop down in beanbags on the bow. I didn't even have to perform the quasi-aerobic maneuver I'd taught myself to use in rough seas so many years ago. A "lift" upon the

T-Top at the crest of a wave to take the disc-compressing bang of a poorly timed or rogue four-to-five-footer.

Eighty-five miles and two and a half hours later, Shannon backed off the throttle as we neared his first spot. The twenty-six-foot Parker settled into the rolling waves, water a clear midnight blue at one hundred and ninety feet. Creeping closer to the structure, Shannon kept a close eye on the electronics on the center console, GPS on the left - sonar on the right.

"There we go …," Shannon said. I looked at the sonar screen. Other than showing a nice patch of fish, it didn't seem that extraordinary to me. "Look at the line at the bottom," he added. Indeed, a thick red border was indicating hard bottom – or limestone. These fields of honeycomb-like surface amid no bottom structure exist everywhere in the Gulf of Mexico – if you know what you're looking for, holes for big snappers and groupers.

Shannon cut the engines. "Aight … Drop 'em." Using heavy rods and reels with five-ounce weights and 5/0 circle hooks, Will, Sidney, and I dropped frozen baits (squid and sardines) one-hundred-and-ninety feet. As soon as they reached the bottom, we were hooked up; red grouper, gag grouper, snapper, but not the big ones yet.

While drifting around, searching for the slot-sized American Red Snapper, in my infinite wisdom, I thought, *Why not break out my heavy baitcasting rig while we're drifting around?* Who of sound mind would be fishing for big snapper with a baitcasting reel and a stout flipping stick, one might ask? Someone from Louisiana, of course, me.

Many anglers avoid baitcasters due to the difficulty of use; the backlash – the dreaded bird's nest. But

he who learneth the skill shall threadeth the needle –
place a lure in a bullseye. Although, offshore there isn't
much to cast to, is there? Regardless, I've caught plenty of cobia, permit, and oversized snook on my heavier
baitcasting tackle. It's been a source of pride over the
years, a redneck purist. But when you're talking about
pig bottom dwellers – well, it's sort of like fishing for
ten-pound carp with a Mickey Mouse rig, which is another story.

In the foreground, I heard a commotion. Sydney
had something big, then so did Will. Shortly after, we
had our first two keeper snapper onboard. "There they
are," said Shannon as he started the engines, moved up,
and engaged the windlass anchor. *"Ddddddddd ...,"* the
twenty-feet of chain attached to the anchor rattled and
clanged its way into the water. Shannon played out anchor rode as he reversed, taking up the slack. The anchor
caught, and the boat swung into position - Easy Like
Sunday Morning.

Shannon is one of a small handful of expert civilian offshore anglers I know. Another being Hill Pohlman
out of Cocodrie, Louisiana. By civilian, I mean nonpro-
fessionals or charter captains. Not only were we catching
fish, but the boatmanship and setup were all-pro. I would
have been circling and pulling anchor and reposition-
ing until I was exhausted, humiliated, and dehydrated –
windlass anchor system notwithstanding.

Now the best course of action would have been
to be better equipped by grabbing some heavier tackle. These were BIG fish that had to come up a LONG
way. Not only did I forgo the conventional wisdom, but
I stood on the rear gunnel with my equivalent to a Mick-

ey Mouse rod and reel, bending my knees, moving with the motion of the ocean. Why I was doing this, I can't remember. I can't remember why I do a lot of the things I do. My step-dad says I'm a hedonist. I had to look that up. Be that as it may, I was getting a bite. I lowered the rod tip closer to the water, all covertly – like the fish could see me. Then …. Gone.

I've cast a rod and reel out of the boat before but recovered it, nearly swept away by the tide in the process. Also, I endangered a good-hearted Boat Club member when she tried to help by retrieving an adrift flip-flop I lost upon the frantic plunge. She leaned over to scoop it up and fell right out of their rented deck boat. That also is another story. On more than one occasion, I've had an unattended rod snatched from the bow of a bay-boat in the marshes of South Louisiana by a lazy redfish. At least once, we recovered the gear by following the popping cork that happened to be tied to it. I want to say the redfish was still on the line as well; I'll have to ask the aforementioned Mr. Pohlman.

However, I have never had a rod and reel vanish from my hands as if summoned by a poltergeist. I looked down in disbelief. I looked to my left to find Sydney's mouth agape and eyes wide. "Did you see that?" I asked her. To which she just busted out laughing. "Stop laughing," I said, "Stop laughing …" Then I started laughing. By now, Will and Shannon were keyed in and were laughing as well.

I could write plain ole fishing stories, but you can read those in the fishing reports and Florida Sportsman and the like. The mishaps, brush-ins, fails, falls, and miscellaneous debauchery that follows me like a shroud of story fodder makes for exciting reading, so I've been told. I'd instead give you something more, such as bond-forging and memory-searing times like these, time and time again.

16

Flip Flop

My last story was an offshore tale, a battle of wills in which I lost to a hungry snapper. Within the content, I mentioned it wasn't the first time I'd gone up against nature, either losing or saving something in the process. This is one of those times.

It was one of those nasty days in the 10,000 Islands when the wind is blowing out of the west, churning up the backwater like the muddy swirls of the Mississippi River, a day that's usually called off. Will (twelve at the time) was here for the summer, Daphne had come to visit, and I was hell-bent on taking them out. Although, I'm pretty sure neither couldn't have cared less.

Conditions far too rough offshore, we limped down the coast in the *Honey Badger "just don't care,"* a 26' center console with twin screws. Not a complicated craft to run for someone with a bit of experience, but none at all… sketchy, boatsman beware.

Anchored in the mouth of a small pass that cut through the center of Cape Romano, soaking shrimp off the stern, I threw my rod and reel out of the boat. No reason, just a disconnect between body and mind.

Abandoning a stationary vessel with passengers not trained to operate it for some of the strongest currents in the state is not recommended. The unrelenting volumes of water rushing in and out of the passes, little rivers, and creeks are not to be underestimated. A couple of other near brushes and stories come to mind. However, my reflexes are faster than my attention span so, out I went as I was, clothes, accessories, and all.

I should mention that I've been a waterman since I was two years old, comfortable in the water and not afraid. The story goes that Mom (Daphne) dropped me off the first day of swimming lessons, *Swimmers by Suzy* – Suzy was teaching kids to swim the length of her pool and back within two weeks. Once the student accomplished the feat, Suzy awarded them with a *Swimmers by Suzy* t-shirt. When Mom picked me up a couple of hours later, I had the T-shirt on, a couple of sizes too big and dragging the floor.

"Jed, why do you already have your shirt on?"

"He's done," Suzy said. "He swam the length of the pool and back today."

I've been bailing out of boats with and without reason ever since.

There is a small window of opportunity in a situation such as this, a point of no return. The rod and reel was moving laterally as fast as it was sinking, the factor that afforded the opportunity because I could see it, barely. I caught the handle at the last minute. Only then did I think about how I was going to get back.

The toes of my right foot managed to clinch around the sandal; the left didn't make it and was already downriver. I reached down, took it off, and compensating for the negative momentum, threw a Hail Mary towards the boat. Doug Flutie himself would've been proud of, end over end it went … Touchdown! I began to make way back with three limbs, the distance growing as I watched. *Uh oh* …, I thought, making no progress. I swam harder. The boat got a little closer. I heard a commotion behind me and turned around to see a lady in a rented pontoon boat fall out as she reached over the side to save my errant flip-flop.

The embarrassment of potentially being the cause of two rescue operations was too much, and I hit the nitrous oxide. Then Will tossed me a life jacket. A valiant move, although strengthening my plight because now I only had two limbs to swim with, my legs, rod and reel in one hand, life jacket in another.

It was now or never, the point of no return where I forfeit my reclaims in exchange for a safe outcome. One last blast of energy put me within a life jacket toss of the boat, which negated some progress, but I made it up, stretching the rod out for Will to grab. Exhausted, I snagged the port side lower unit, pulled myself to the stern, folded the swim ladder down, and climbed up.

A small crowd had formed on the beach on the north side of the pass. I heard a few claps and cheers. The woman was safe back aboard the rental, flip-flop in hand, and my sunglasses were still around my neck. Other than having a salty reel to clean, everything was in place.

If you're going to be dumb, you better be tough.

17

He's Doing It Again

Anchored off the sandy beach of a barrier island south of Cocodrie, Louisiana, we were in them thick. Speckled trout, all sizes - hand over fist - we whacked 'em.

Hill Pohlman, a buddy close enough to call my brother, had a Bay Hawk at the time, which had poorly designed scuppers that sat low in the stern and allowed water to pool in the hull while the boat was at rest. Within the flaw, however, was a silver lining in the form of a makeshift live well. Therefore, we unhooked them and dropped them into the boat, saving time and catching more fish.

It may be hard to understand for someone that has never experienced it, but the rush of getting into a ravenous bite such as this is part of what it's all about. The angler and sportsman in us are on a never-ending quest to duplicate the experience. Not as intense as playing in a football game that your team is winning, but close. Everyone is hooting and hollering and high-fiving.

Coming from Florida, I wasn't used to the 12" minimum size for speckled trout. Therefore, I took a break and began tossing the smaller ones out. Hill witnessed my efforts and stammered, "Hhhhey, man! Hey, man! Wwwe're kkeepin em all … we're keepin em all!"

Larue, the big guy with a deep voice, emphasized Hill's statement in his Mississippi drawl, "Yeah … We're keepin em all." (A Mississippi drawl is different from a North Louisiana Drawl or a Texas twang. Southern ears denote that difference.)

"Even these dinks?" I asked.

"I want some fish in the freezer," Larue said, confirming the demand. Twenty-five per person bag limit with five people. Let's see …, I learned algebra from Granny, same as Jethro. That's … a lot of fish. Every one of them was cleaned and iced to be shared and enjoyed by all of us with freezers. For some reason, I felt like I needed to clarify that.

"Tttwelve inches, Man. Twelve inches," Hill said, reminding me of the starting slot size.

When excited, Hill stutters and stammers, spewing jumbled sentences, sometimes inventing new phrases in the process. He has ever since we were kids. It was so funny we would often provoke or bring on these bouts of silliness. It became a favorite past-time, all in good fun. As you will soon see, I was usually the one getting hazed, which is why I waited a few minutes and started again.

I bumped into Thomas, another childhood friend close enough to be a brother, while sloshing around, making a spectacle chasing fish around. "Dude …," Thomas says, alerting Hill in deep concentration on the bow. Hill turned around to find me chase a particularly slippery one around Taylor's legs, catch it, and throw it out. Taylor - Larue's son, a spritely teen at the time.

"LLLarue! Larue! Hhhe's dddoing it again! He's doing it again!"

"Boy … Don't let me see you do that again, or I'm gonna throw YOU out of the boat," said Larue. Only his voice seemed much deeper at this point.

Hill was wild-eyed, unable to think of anything to stammer. I read the dare on Thomas and Taylor's faces and knew I had no choice. Picking up the biggest trout I could find, I moved closer to Larue so that he got a good look and let it slide over the side.

I didn't have time to think to myself – "*He's not kidding*" - before I was in the water. I may have beaten the fish I had tossed out – it was close. I dog paddled around while they laughed at me, all the while they continued to catch fish.

You see, Larue was a man of his word. He never wore a wristwatch and did deals on a handshake. If he said, "Don't touch the radio," or, "Don't let me see you do that again, or I'm going to throw you out of the boat," he meant it. Thomas can attest to the former.

I'm now vividly reminded of the harrowing game of Duck - Duck - "who's going to get the electric fillet knife with a short in it," that Larue and I played later that afternoon. A slight jolt every few seconds for the length of time it takes to clean a fair share of 125 speckled trout, plus a good haul of redfish can be maddening. I lost.

Issuing this clarification postscript was important to preserve the integrity of the original story I pulled from, "Big Guy With The Deep Voice," eulogizing my dear friend, Larue Byrd. Also, within the story is the spirit of "Pop," Mr. Jimmy Pohlman, an essential figure in my younger life.

18

10,000 Islands Christmas

I could smell the ripeness of the exposed marine life as I began to stir – the scent of marine borers, alive and decaying matter mixed. Christmas morning didn't bring hot cocoa and a warm fire. Not this year; this year it brought a low tide and a favorable forecast. There was anticipation but not from gifts awaiting under the tree but from fish awaiting under the mangrove roots.

The wind had been 10-15 knots out of the west for the last two days, churning up Barfield Bay like margaritas in a blender, choppy and unpredictable. I jumped the 17' Maverick tunnel hull up on plane and rode the chop, standing up at the helm. The water slipped over the gunnel each time I fell out of rhythm, yet the cool sting of the saltwater spray felt fresh and invigorating as opposed to harsh and punishing.

Upon reaching the end of the no wake zone in Goodland it occurred to me that I had recognized and obeyed the dreaded "Slow Speed Manatee Zones," an act I had previously disregarded. How could I have forgotten standing before a judge in a federal court room in Fort Myers after receiving a fourth violation? "How in the hell does a West Indian Manatee know where it's safe and where it isn't?" I pleaded. The judge didn't think much of my argument.

I banked around Tripod Key and began the backwater route that served as the mental illusion for the "relaxation techniques" I had learned at marriage counseling several years earlier. They didn't help one bit with my marriage, but it had always worked to ease my mind during stressful times. I imagine every point and every turn I pass along the way. "I can navigate these waters blindfolded," I would often claim. Could that statement be a bit of an exaggeration? Possibly, be that as it may, I can navigate these waters in the dark with the occasional shine of a light no problem. The meandering mangrove route is forever ingrained in my mind.

Buttonwood Bay is my favorite spot in all the 10,000 islands. Buttonwood is dangerously shallow at low tide with jagged oyster bars lurking around every turn. Not knowing their locations could easily result in ripping out a lower unit. Good luck if that happens because no one is coming; I speak from experience.

Fishermen are creatures of habit, and I began my pattern at the same spot where I always had, a spot I named simply, The Oyster Bar. I quietly unfastened and released the trolling motor, easing it down into the tannic water. I began trolling parallel to the bar making calculated casts as close as possible without getting hung on the rough shells. My lure fell into an eddy created by two adjoining oyster points – "Bang! Hello Mr. Redfish."

Pushing a button on a lanyard around my neck, I engaged the Power Pole, a shallow water anchor. I could hear the buzz of the mechanism and a crunch as the fiberglass rod was shoved into the broken-up oyster shells and detritus that had flowed from the everglades for thousands of years. I was then fixed in place, free to work the area thoroughly.

There was a deep point on the west side that, at times, held big gator speckled trout. With a strong flick of the wrist I made a long side armed cast out across the point and let my jig sink to the bottom before making slow twitches of the rod tip. On my second cast I felt the telltale slight bump of a speckled trout taking the bait. I swept the rod to the side so as not to jerk the hook out the fish's soft mouth. Sure enough, the specs were there and hungry.

The sky had begun to redden but I had one more spot to try. *I hope I have enough water to get out*, I thought as I pulled the trolling motor up, ran down the wide gunnels, and jumped down onto the bench seat. The trim was set just right and with speed the Maverick danced on top of a light chop that had formed in the bay. A few seconds later I cut the engine and hurried to the bow, snatching my baitcaster along the way. I could see activity as the boat rode its own wake, coasting towards the mouth of Whitney River. I tossed the jig up current and let it fall, sweeping past the point of the river mouth. "Bang!" The big red nearly jerked the rod out of my hand. After several minutes I horsed the fish alongside the boat, popped the jig out of its mouth, and boxed it. A perfect way to end a perfect day.

The sun had fallen lower on the horizon, the sky resembled the tin roof on an ancient barn, rusted red. The bay had calmed, reflecting the same color off of the water, making it difficult to distinguish surface from sky. One swift punch of the throttle and I began the journey back in the fading light. The evening was still and calm, the air crisp, and the water glass. There was no movement in the trees, no ripple of nervous bait, not a soul for miles... I caught the blurred reflection of a "Slow Speed Manatee Zone" as I bypassed Goodland, speeding through the Everglades, in the dark.

19

Well, Do You Feel Lucky?

Drifting across a sandy shoal pocketed with coral and seagrass off Turtle Key, water a pale turquoise, neither clear nor muddy, I thought, *this is the day I wash the redfish skunk off me.* With a character on board named "Lucky," how could I spend another day on the water without catching one? The law of averages? Something must give.

Trout, snook, snapper, pompano, tripletail, tarpon sometimes – I did alright. Catching speckled trout has inadvertently become my "thing," per se. Not as sexy to some, but there's a player for every position. Not everyone can be quarterback, but it's better to be the punter than not make the team. In the spirit of such, I embraced the snaggle-toothed bait thumpers. But the fact that I had not been able to catch a redfish in months had become a problem.

Being a student of the game, striking out on reds time and time again was a source of anxiety and personal dissatisfaction. Also, I was tired of avoiding the topic of conversation with one of my compadres, an offshore guide, and a trusted proofreader, Drake. He'd commented, something to the effect that I should get a redfish tattooed *somewhere* where I could at least see one when I used the bathroom. This must stop.

My enthusiasm remained steadfast even after Will, my son, politely informed Lucky that the spinning reel he was holding was upside down. A common mistake among those unfamiliar with certain types of fishing tackle. Lucky grew up in Iowa, known more for wrestlers than anglers. When he moved to Florida, he told me he had to choose between an airplane or a boat. The plane was cheaper. The faux pas was understandable, and we didn't tease him too much.

Lucky is my friend and landlord. I responded to an ad for a condo on Marco in which Lucky (I think that might be his name. I haven't asked) quickly and exuberantly replied. A few minutes later, it felt like we were old friends. This ability being a common trait among successful salesmen, it came as no surprise to learn he is one of the top realtors on an island of hundreds. The proof is in the unobstructed view clear to the Yucatan from his condo high above Caxambas Pass.

Loyalty to my friends sometimes comes at a price. Yet, in my experience, the price is always worth it. For instance, do I want to complain to my Amigo that hot air is funneling through the old glazing and shutter system? Or that birds have taken residence in the ceiling? I did complain about that one, and he put in a work order. In the meantime, I came to realize there were no birds but a squeaky ceiling fan. I've been too embarrassed to disclose the revelation. I can hear his charismatic, bellowing laugh as he reads this. Surprise!

"What's that?" asked Lucky in response to the information Will had given him regarding the upside-down reel. Before anyone could respond, a crafty ladyfish or a sprinting jack took a swipe at the live shrimp on the end of his line, flipping the reel over. "Oh…" replied Lucky, "Ha! How about that!"

"Leave it there for a minute. If your shrimp isn't gone, something might come back and get it," I said, whipping a jig side-armed with both hands as far as I could to reach the cut on the edge of the shoal. Suddenly, Lucky's popping cork disappeared, and his line began moving sideways at a rapid rate of speed. Although, he'd yet to feel the pull on the end of the line. "Uh…" Will said, "I think you've got one."

Lucky reeled in the slack, the rod bowed, and the drag started peeling off the reel. "Oh boy, do I ever!"

"Yes, you do," I replied, laying my rod down, scrambling for the Boga Grip, getting ready to land the fish should the fight go Lucky's way. I didn't say anything, but the way the fish fought, pulling steady amidst blistering runs, led me to believe that he had a nice red. *Yes! I knew it,* I thought, still keeping the idea to myself. My behavior was indicative of the silly superstitions in which anglers are sometimes governed. Although, it wouldn't have mattered because the bruiser ended up being a colossal jack crevalle.

We moved around the outer islands, catching a little bit of everything; small snook, mangrove snapper, and slot size trout were the A-Listers of the day. Trash fish bit and pulled on our lines, providing much entertainment, but they don't count.

Following the incoming tide into the backwater, trolling from point to point, fishing the deeper holes that hold gator trout in the cooler months, we picked up one here, two there as we went.

The tide was rushing over a massive oyster ridge towards the back of a bay that I'm choosing to remain nameless. I cast to the edge where my jig became snagged. I popped the line a couple of times using what I call the Ole Banjo Trick. With slack line, I pulled out an arms-length and snapped it several times. Not unlike a fast version of drawing a compound bow and slinging an arrow. The vibration ran down the line to the lure, pushing it off its snag.

That one always garnishes looks of surprise for those who've never seen it. This time was no different. Lucky looked at me wild-eyed. "Old Louisiana bass fishing technique," I said. I barely got the comment out when something peeled off the oyster bar and took off with my jig. I set the hook and tried to turn the fish away from the oyster bar, but "Pop!" the line broke. "Well," I said, "That was my redfish. Or a tripletail." Oddly, I've caught several of the crab-pot loiterers in this particular backwater bay.

Although the redfish continued to elude me, we had a spectacular day. A box full of trout and a few keeper snapper. Memories made, a bond strengthened, and a friendship solidified was lucky enough for me. As we rounded the corner at Tripod Key, the sun was low on the horizon in line with Caxambas Pass, an orange orb hovering directly above Lucky's place.

20

Redtile Dysfunction

It's no laughing matter that fifty-five percent of anglers suffer from Redtile Dysfunction at some point within their fishing tenure. Redtile dysfunction is a generic term used to describe the inability of an angler to catch the targeted species over an extended time. Which defines my struggles as I continue the quest to catch a redfish, as documented in my last story, *"Well, Do You Feel Lucky?"*

One must remember that it's ok to ask for help, which is what I did when I invited my friend, and former Estero Bay guide, Sean Davis, to come fishing with me out of Goodland, my home base. Sean is a live bait fisherman and a popping cork enthusiast, arguably the most productive method to fish this region, and pretty much the exact opposite style as mine. Perfect scenario to breathe life into my red drum doldrums.

The problem with live bait, aside from shrimp, which are sold live at most marinas, is that it's not always around. Depending on the time of year and a myriad of conditions, a fisherman can spend hours chasing baitfish while the peak fishing time comes and goes. Or one might toss their cast net smooth out of the boat and wrap it around Coon Key Light. I will use live bait provided I can find it quickly, and I almost always buy a few dozen shrimp. However, I primarily use artificial lures. Trolling along, making strategic casts is more my game.

The exercise was to load up with shrimp, get out there, and for Sean to tell me what he'd do differently. Ultimately, other than pointing out several spots I hadn't thought to try, Sean thought my methods were sound. We caught some of everything, including a limit of speckled trout but no redfish. Sean outfished me, but not by much. Man, I had no idea how many ways a popping cork can be used. I spend more time keeping the slack out of my line, whereas Sean will let that line sag like a loaded clothesline as long as the bait is within the strike zone.

Later, back at Dad's dock cleaning fish, I had a moment of clarity. *How could this have slipped my mind?* My dilemma could be explained by The Pohlman Theory, which states that, on average, an angler's claim is seldom wholly accurate. It seems that everyone I talk to is catching reds as of late. Then I thought long and hard, narrowing it down to (3). I've spoken to a total of three people who told me they'd caught redfish. But had they?

Hill Pohlman, featured in my story, "He's Doing It Again," is a lifelong friend and angler extraordinaire. Much of what I know I learned from him. But Hill gets excited and acts erratically once the bite is on. At the end of the day, he couldn't tell you exactly how many fish he had caught. In South Louisiana, you can lose count quick. The element of typical angler bravado and Hill's notorious embellishment was the basis for our profound theory.

Being the Einstein of angler BS, I realized a pattern was not mutually exclusive to bag limits but in all sportsmen's assertions. A few of us like-minded individuals got together and went to work with the proper funding; collecting data, studying psychological behavior patterns, and formulating theoretical equations resulted in a revolutionary discovery in human behavior. An integer assigned to quantities, size, and productive areas to reveal a more honest number, The Pohlman Unit is .314.

Let me break it down. On average, 30% of anglers inflate their declarations. "Ahh, we ripped 'em, caught 20." Factor in the Pohlman Unit, 20 x .314 = 6.28. Take that off the total, and the result is a more realistic number - 13.7 fish. Remember that 30% is an average. Some stories, such as the one I just told about the Pohlman Units, can be up to 90% untrue.

Case in point, I told Dad we caught twenty trout. But per The Pohlman Theory, it was more like fourteen. The justification was that a couple of big ones got off at the boat, and we missed several strikes.

The moral here is that I may be too hard on myself (no pun intended). There's at least a 30% chance that I may not be catching any redfish because they're all in Estero Bay. It could be that only a handful of anglers have been catching reds. Hell, I may not need a blue pill after all. We'll have to see, won't we, Amigos?

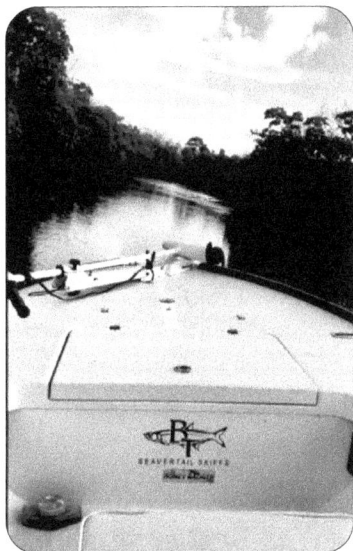

21

How Dare You...

I watched George as he sat across from me, elbows on the desk in my office, weathered face bordered by a thick white mustache contorted in thought as he made his marks. When he finished, he stood up, handed me the chart, and said, "There ya go, Bo." A native South Florida Cracker, he said: "snuke," instead of "snook," more like "nuke" than "book."

You see? George Smith was one of the greatest sportsmen I've known. His list of accolades is too long for a short story, inventing the willow leaf spinnerbait being among the least impressive. For George to share this knowledge with me was huge.

Many years later, I understand that chart is among the greatest gifts I've ever received. I still have it somewhere, along with a slate turkey call with a wooden strike tied to it he gave me. The marks George made were like pieces to an actual scale jigsaw puzzle. Each spot I learned made the picture a little clearer. These were my directions for the 10,000 Islands.

I studied it, memorized routes and landmarks - it's all downloaded in my mind. Armed with the Golden Scroll shoved under my leg, referencing it along the way like a "slide rule" version of the modern GPS map, I ventured out. When GPS mapping systems became standard equipment, I found that I barely used them. Since then, I have used the technology to expand my knowledge, but I learn the terrain.

Anyone with a skinny water vessel can follow a GPS track anywhere. That would take some of the pleasure out of it for me. There is nothing more serene to me than moving freely through that maze of mangroves without having to think about which way to turn. Negotiating hull-ripping oyster bars hidden at high tide and avoiding hazards at every turn by memory, not glued to a screen, is liberating. I tell people they'll never learn the area until they turn that thing off – part of the time.

There are many thousands of acres yet to learn… I don't know if anyone can learn all the 10,000 Islands. But the little swaths here and there that are still a bit uncomfortable, I make a point to travel whenever possible, adding another piece to the puzzle. I'll try to find my way, and should I get turned around - a slightly lesser version of being lost, I'll reference the GPS. Well, my GPS hasn't worked for about eight months … I haven't been too concerned about it. If I ever need to know my location, I use my phone. This finally sets the stage for what happened a few weeks ago in what ended up being the Dismal River.

This instance was particularly confusing in its simplicity, just a slightly different route from point A to point B than usual. Once you begin to question your location, things become disorientating; perception is skewed - depth expands and contracts, and time is warped. Pretty soon, the only way to know which way is up is to follow the bubbles, a fail-safe for SCUBA divers. However, I knew that I knew where I was. I just didn't know yet. My location was on the tip of my tongue like lyrics to a song you can't think of the title for. So, I kept riding, looking for my landmarks. After a good try, I backed down to idle in a wide body of water - some river. I took my phone out and pinpointed my location. I looked left and right, then behind me… *I'll be dang. I knew it!* In an instant, my bearings returned to the Dismal River. In that vertigo-like state, I'd traveled twice the distance that it had seemed.

Suddenly, I heard a vessel approaching from behind and moving fast. I made sure I was not in any blind spot and that I was safely over to the right side near the entrance to a small bay that had a sand/mudflat at the mouth. Suddenly, the boat was upon me, passing too close on my starboard side. In passing came a muffled yell through a neck gator. I didn't make out what the operator said, but I didn't need to. I heard the arrogance and sarcasm ebbing and flowing through the wind and the sound of our outboard motors as he sped by, a fly-fishing guide outfitted with all the latest garb in matching saltwater camo. I can always spot the guides. They'll look a little different from everyone else aboard, in this case, just the one passenger, appearing slightly out of place.

The comment had something to do with the fact that I was looking at my phone; *Get off your phone, you idiot, pay attention to what you're doing...,* something like that. Like I was among the hordes of personal water-craft that have launched an amphibious assault on Marco Island with reckless abandon and nonexistent common mariner courtesies. That topic deserves its own story.

I looked around to see who he was talking to. There was nobody else. *"I know he's not talking to me... He must not know who he's talking to. This is MY Point Break."* The Hell's Bay Luxury Poling Skiff settled in its wake well inside the bay, presumably looking for tailing redfish. *"Someone ought to tell him,"* I thought as I followed him, pushing a nasty wake.

I wasn't on Instagram, or FaceBook, or TicTac, or Slipchat. But what if I was? What if I was texting my high school girlfriend, who I ran into at the Marriott the weekend prior, reminiscing about things only first loves can? Who is this guy to bludgeon my serenity? The wave runners are bad enough.

As the distance closed, I began seeing red, fighting mad. "What was that?" I hollered once I was within hearing distance. He pulled the buff down and said something about letting me know that he was passing. I could tell that he wasn't accustomed to being called out for being rude; most people that are prone to being a-holes aren't. I proceeded to tell him that he was full of S and that he was being a smart-ass. The conversation got heated, so I moved closer, thinking, *"Good grief, this is going to turn into a good old-fashioned dust-up like on the Homasassa Flats during the tarpon record craze of the '70s....'* Stories of Billy Pate and Tom Evans came to mind. He's yelling, I'm yelling... Then my forward momentum was stalled. I looked behind and saw the mud in my wake.

In my agitated state, I hadn't noticed that I'd drifted on the sand bar; a good thing in that the confrontation was stymied. I'd like to think that it wouldn't have gone any further, but that would have depended on him. I was committed to my ignorance; we're talking pride and ego here. I trimmed up the motor and jack-plate and eased away not as quickly as I'd come, churning up the bottom. I must say, the prospect of running aground after such a display was the worst part by far. I don't fear any man, but humiliation scares the hell out of me.

Players of the same game just opposite sides; I'd be willing to bet if we meet again, we'd share a good laugh. I've made more than a few friends through conflict, trivial variety especially. As a matter of fact, Capt. Saltwater Camo, if you read this, hit me up at jedmls@mac.com. Let's go get a beer.

As this story concludes, it occurs to me that I should probably go ahead and get my GPS fixed.

22

Four on Five

Standing with a broad base, I leaned into the turns. Curlews spooked as I rounded the mangrove bends as if I'd caught them at something. They look guilty or embarrassed to me; the Chokoloskee Chickens do – aka curlews. Maybe it's their laborious gait in flight.

I came to a shallow water bay, straightened the skiff, and opened the throttle. Herons stood in the mud facing the incoming water, waiting for dinner. The mid-morning sun cast a glare off the water, blinding me in intervals, like heading East on 635 in Dallas, Texas, on a clear morning. I couldn't see the ditches and troughs that otherwise reveal themselves in a meandering trail of darker water. I followed the same path as always. I didn't need to see them.

The low rumble of my outboard motor was like white noise from a sleep machine. My head nodded but snapped to when the bow began to hop. The saltwater splashed evenly off the forward beam, "ssshhppsshhh," "ssshhppsshhh," "ssshhppsshhh." I pushed two buttons on the right side of the gunnel that controlled the hydraulic trim tabs underneath the transom. Once… twice… one more little bump, and the boat flattened out.

There was a small opening on the eastern end of the bay that led to a series of sharp turns, ending at the mouth of a small creek that served as a shortcut to the Turtle Key/Dismal Key Pass area. A GPS screen shows a black skull and crossbones – do not navigate. Therefore, during any stage of the tide besides high, trimmed out, jacked up, and hauling ass is the only way to pass. Or else a rapid loss of forward momentum can occur. It's called "running aground," I write about it frequently. I don't recommend it.

The creek, or shortcut, was tucked behind a hairpin left – a blind spot. Detritus from storms past littered the flat off to the right; therefore, I swung wide and hugged the mangrove bank. Hunkered down, no standing for this one, I pulled the tiller handle in as far as I could, contorting my left shoulder behind my back, and cut the turn. There they were, Craig Cats, moving about aimlessly like the traffic on Marco in March, ignorant to the complexity of the terrain with no idea of the navigational difficulties. Fists waved, and mouth holes moved as I rode around them in a cloverleaf pattern like a quarter horse in a barrel race. In my peripheral vision, I saw their guide scold them and do his best to usher them out of the way, which gave me hope for humanity. Due to his efforts and my kitty-cat nimbly reflexes, we narrowly avoided an accident.

The ones that aren't led by a tour guide are easy to spot, zipping from one end of a bay to the other, throwing a wake against anyone who might be soaking up some tranquility wetting a line. One day, after the third or fourth pass, whipping up the water like a wave pool, a gaggle of WaveRunners slowed down enough to ask me which direction was Marco Island. I haphazardly pointed west on shaky sea legs, the trolling motor cavitating at the top of every wake they'd pushed. I wonder if they ever made it out? Should anyone be missing any family members, there's a clue.

Craig Cat is among the class of personal watercraft, along with the more common WaveRunner, that has inundated the traditionally unmolested backwaters of the 10,000 islands. Clumsy by design, the catamarans resemble paddleboards cut in half and fastened together by what is effectively the seat and footrest for two people. Powered by a 25 hp outboard mounted high on a make-shift transom and a Bimini top to shield the rider from the sun, they appear top-heavy as a weeble-wobble.

When I lived on the Caloosahatchee River, my next-door neighbor, Dick, had one. Ole' Dick looked like the scary man in Poltergeist who knocked on the door and told everyone, "You're all gonna die." Why he had a Craig Cat is beyond me, not that ghostly-looking figures can't partake in water sports. Yet 10 yards up the seawall from my duplex, his Craig Cat sat high up on a rickety boat lift with rusted cables.

I came in from fishing one afternoon and made a 180 in the canal when I passed my house to begin "walking" my old jon-boat towards the seawall like always. I backed off the throttle to reverse to starboard… no re-

sponse. Disregarding neutral, I slammed it in reverse…
no response. The throttle cable had broken in its forward
position, "Boom!" The blow was glancing and shot me
down the seawall like an aluminum eight ball in the corner pocket that was Dick's pier. As the bunk boards of
the boat lift became closer and closer at eye level, impact
was imminent. I ducked at the last fraction of a second
as they passed over me. I snatched the kill switch, cutting power amidst a series of crashes as my boat went
ping-ponging around underneath the lift.

My neighbors on the opposite side of Dick, Heinz
and Laura, were outside and witnessed the debacle. "Are
you alright?" They asked frantically as the flimsy dock
settled on its decrepit piles. I rose from my crouched position, poked my head up, and replied in quick breaths,
"Did you see that?" Dick opened the door to his back
porch and asked, "What was that?" Not in the literal
sense, but more like asking for something to be repeated.
Assessing the damage, which there appeared to be none,
I replied, "All good here, Dick." He went back inside.

It's a good thing I inherited fast reflexes. Daphne,
my mom, was a majorette at Louisiana Tech and falling
grocery juggler extraordinaire to this day. I once saw her
catch four cans in Brookshires, West Monroe, La, circa
1982. Big curly hair, wind shorts, leggings, and white
Rebook High Tops, she reached up on her tiptoes high
enough to get a finger on a can of Cream of Mushroom.
She caught it when it dropped, as intended. Another fell
into the same right hand, "Pow!" With quickness, she
juked and snagged another one in her left hand, "Bang!"

By now, a crowd had formed, consisting mainly
of men. For the finale, she twirled and let the fourth fall

in her hands behind her back, "Booya!" Aisle Five erupted in cheers.

23

Nice Gainer

I was wrapping up the laborious process of preparing for a journey such as the one I was about to embark on when my 17' Beavertail Skiff fell off the boat lift. I know it did because I was standing in it when it happened.

Once or twice per year, it has become a tradition for me to head out into the 10,000 Islands for a couple of days by myself. Initially, being alone wasn't my intention, but none of my fishing compadres were interested. A short list to begin with, as there are but a few souls I would consider partaking in such an outing. I didn't need anyone to hold my hand, so alone I went. Since then, it has become somewhat of a tradition, my annual walkabout, my "solo," spiritual recharging, and homage to Gods of the Everglades.

It appeared as if I would miss it this year, as I usually go mid-winter. However, Easter weekend presented perfect conditions and an opportunity. The wind finally laid down, and the evening temperature was still a little cooler than the average household, the calm before the insect storm. Anyone who has been stranded somewhere inundated with no-see-ums understands the significance of this. If hell is worse, I should consider repenting for a lifetime of excesses and debauchery.

The lift, although adequate capacity, is better suited for personal watercraft than it is a flats boat. Although with a few modifications, it works just fine, and has for the combined five years I've kept a vessel the size of mine in it. However, the wooden bunks are positioned so that a boat with a beam width such as mine leans slightly to the left, sometimes more than others, making it seem unstable. Thus, I formulated a habit of walking around gingerly and making soft movements. I've never even come close to tipping over.

Common practice is to remove the plugs after loading a boat, whether onto a trailer or lift, allowing water that the bilge may have missed to drain. The plugs stay out until the next trip so that the hull doesn't accumulate moisture, especially from the freshwater washdowns saltwater boats go through. However, unbeknownst to me, in my infinite wisdom, I had forgotten to take the plugs out following my last outing. Therefore, water from two full wash downs, plus one or two rain events, was sitting in the hull, concentrated on the leaning left side.

Cognizant of the hazard, yet ignorant of the extra water weight, I made a point not to step too far on that side as I directed the stream of water towards the port bow, pushing the last of the suds over the edge. A catastrophe was the furthest thing from my mind as I watched the bubbles fall and listened to the tinkle of the water below, oblivious of the grave danger upon me and that my reaction in the following fraction of a second would ultimately determine my fate.

The port side rolled on its x-axis 90 degrees and fell off of the lift, like a trap door opening beneath me, dumping me into the water. "*This isn't going to be good for anybody*," I thought as the brisk water took my breath.

There wasn't time to think. My brain registered that the volume of space required for the mass that had to occupy it was less than the sum of the two masses - my boat and myself. The point where the dock and seawall met formed a triangle, with the "A" leg being the only way out towards the canal and deeper water - which was the direction I was headed when the boat rolled over onto my shoulders, a heavy "thud" pushing me into the sandy bottom.

The craft's weight in the water reduced the impact to a violent push as opposed to blunt force trauma. The buoyancy prevented the hull from pinning me to the surface, allowing me to swim from under it. I dog-paddled around in shock, looking to see if there had been a witness. Nobody was around; nobody saw the event; everything was quiet. I swam to the seawall and managed to climb up at mid-tide, not an easy feat. The cuts on my hands, arms, feet, and legs from the barnacles are proof.

Some say that I have bad luck. Saying that I don't concur at times would be slightly untrue. Although, when broken down to the total number of risky activities divided by the number of "bad luck" events, the ratio is appropriate – theoretically speaking, as the divisor is a considerable number. As a humble critic, I will admit that if near misses were a category, I couldn't say the same.

I've partaken in more dangerous endeavors than the average person since the 80s growing up as a skater. Not a skateboarder, but a skater – there's a difference. One doesn't progress at the sport without being able to compartmentalize fear. No guts, no glory became a mantra.

Being a skater was more than riding a board with wheels. It was an attitude. Anti-establishment with a seething opposition to authority; we were athletes not governed by groups, teams, leagues, or coaches, yet athletes, nonetheless. Before the modern age of skateparks, skateboarding was a crime. If there was an obstacle worthy of skating, we skated it. No trespassing signs we were blind to; security guards we ran from; and in police stations and college security offices we sat. Like it or not, taking risks is part of my DNA.

> *"I don't want to not live because of my fear of what could happen."*
> —*Laird Hamilton*

24

Salesman of the Year

I'm not sure what it is about anglers rooted in bass fishing that requires us to have more rods and reels than anyone could use in a given day. That said, I motioned to the egregious display I'd placed aboard and shouted over the noise of the outboard motor, "Which do you prefer?" When Woody pointed to a baitcaster, I knew it would be a good day.

Why did such a thing fire my positivity receptors? Because anyone comfortable enough to choose baitcasting over spinning tackle is a practiced caster. Enough said. If fishing tackle were golf clubs, baitcasters were the long irons, hardest to hit, but with practice, and some natural ability, deadly accurate.

Nici grabbed a cold Michelob Ultra from the ice chest, popped the top, blew the foam off with one big, *pppfff,* then took a swig. "This is the fourth year in a row he's been nominated for Salesman of the Year," she said in the sweetest southern drawl you've ever heard. She wore a baseball cap on top of hair so dark it was almost black, had the face of an angel, and hazel eyes that said, "I'm Nici, and you want to know me."

"So, you're like the Susan Lucci of the Auto Parts Industry?" I asked Woody, Nici's husband.

"Susan Coochie?" said Woody, in the deepest southern drawl you've ever heard, as he fired a cast that skipped once, twice, then fell into the little pocket between two mangrove branches. The water blew up with a loud *gulppop*! A flash of silver cut a swath through the tannic water. The fish jumped and skipped along the surface on its tail before making a run back to its tangled lair.

"Nice snook!" I said. With tight line, Woody pulled to the side, holding the rod against his body, and turned the fish. "That's why I like bringing good old boys from back home fishing!" I said, moving nimbly around the boat, getting ready to land the fish. By "back home," I mean Louisiana and Mississippi. "That's how it's done! This is your year, Woody!" He fought the fish a little longer and brought it in so I could clamp the Boga-Grip (fish grappler) around its lip. I missed, and the fish got off, thus ruining a photo op.

We trolled down the bank against the current, making strategic casts around points, pockets, and little inlets. We talked and laughed, caught fish, got broken off, and I nearly fell in - a common occurrence..

Woody landed several smaller snook, and I caught a bruiser similar to his I let get away. He fought fiercely with honor as snook always do, sending me around the boat to the bow, where I had to shove the rod halfway underwater to avoid getting caught in the trolling motor.

This is a call for everyone to put their devices down, get outside, and do something cool with people. The world will be a better place, I promise. The wilderness is my sanctuary, and mother nature is my higher power. Zinging drags, the slap of high-fives and braided line whistling back through guides are gospel to my ears. Out here, differences are put aside amidst ebb and neap tides where bonds are formed, respect is earned, and relationships are built among the most unlikely of characters. Where else would one end up taking their ex-girlfriend's husband fishing, along with said girlfriend? That's right, Nici was my high school sweetheart.

The sun was low over Marco Island, and through the rain clouds on the horizon, the sky looked bruised. Quickly I pulled the trolling motor out of the water, folded it down, and wiggled my way to the engine to get to the Snook Inn before the deluge. Nici wanted to get her dad a t-shirt, hopefully similar to the one she brought him back in 1991 when she and I came down to the Island for vacation.

Woody won the Salesman of the Year award, by the way.

25

Ride It Out

I'll put this cloud behind me
That's how the man designed me
To ride the wind and dance in a hurricane
—Keith Whitley

I realized I had something moments after reading the assignment for last month's Marco Island Writer's Guild meeting. *"A challenge to our writing members: 500 words, more or less, on the subject of Hurricane Ian."* Getting a message across in a few words - that's my game, so I've been told. As vague images of a story sneaked in and out of my mind, I scanned the email again to confirm I hadn't read anything specific regarding non-fiction or fiction, as what was brewing was no doubt fantasy.

The concept was this: theoretically, the eye of Hurricane Ian could have just as easily come ashore here, on Marco, instead of Fort Myers Beach. In my case, 1,000 feet from the beach. To further theorize, the storm could have come ashore during a stronger tide and closer to the top of that tide. Throw in an X and Y factor, intensifying the strength, and my short piece is well beyond the realm of possibility.

Therefore, I wrote it but didn't show up for the meeting. Not because I didn't want to, but because I did something that many people suffering from Bi-Polar disorder do and blew off an activity better left unblown. However, because my editors, Lynn and Kathy, are super cool, they published it here. Hopefully, my fellow Guild Members will catch the issue.

Those 500 words are as follows:

From my second-story bedroom window, I watched tropical detritus and building materials of all kinds fly by as if blown by a Husqvarna Blower the size of the Super Dome. I tapped on the newly installed storm windows and was glad that Greg, the best window guy on the Island, won the bid to install new windows in the Seabreeze Complex. Many a hurricane I've sat through, but never one that lingered so long, smashing Marco Island for hours with vicious right hooks, pushing the Gulf of Mexico directly towards us.

When the storm finally passed, one foot of water stood in the parking lot. I walked on to the balcony, where a series of ropes hung from the roof that I had secured. Stepping on the balcony rail, I pulled myself up and walked to the western edge for a better view. The water in the parking lot had grown several feet. I looked toward the beach, only 1000 feet away but out of sight due to the mega condos that owned the airspace. You can imagine the anxiety, when through a wide gap in the nearest two condos, I thought I saw the silvery tips of waves. *Impossible,* I thought, *that would be like Waimea Bay breaking on Tigertail Beach,"* yet the perpetually rising tide below slapped me with reality.

I hustled back down, grabbed the two bags I'd placed inside the door, and hooked them up to my ropes. One bag was a floating waterproof backpack containing provisions for a couple of days, a first aid kit and insect repellent. The other was my USAF Pararescue (PJ's) gear bag. I hadn't prepared for a power outage, nor did I stock up on weeks' worth of supplies. I never intended on sticking around long enough to need them. I prepared to attempt to survive a potentially catastrophic storm surge of biblical proportions.

Wasting no time, I pulled on my wetsuit, booties, hood, gloves, and chest protector and strapped dive knives to both ankles. The water had risen to the point that I could see it coming in the distance. The first floor was inundated and rising. As I strapped on my helmet, I understood what it must have felt like standing on a rooftop in the Lower Ninth Ward when the Industrial Canal levee wall failed and let the Mississippi River pour in.

I watched other structures being pushed off their foundations as floating debris slammed into the building and violent vortexes swirled around the corners. As the surge reached roof level, I pulled on my backpack and ran to the eastern edge, where I sat in several inches of water and secured my SCUBA fins over my booties. The condo shifted beneath me, and I jumped, angling for the highest point on the island, Indian Hill, deep inside Caxambas Pass.

"Ride it Out" was no longer a cliché. It was my harsh realm.

That concludes my 500 words. Although, I had more in my head, such as riding a wayward crane boom like a giant surge dragon and grabbing hold of the roof parapet of the last house on the Island before being dragged deep into the 10,000 Islands. Fodder for a longer story, I suppose.

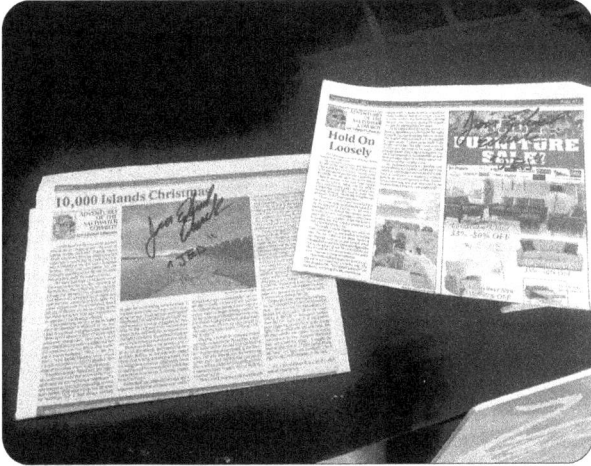

26

Biggest Fan

I sat alone in the back row of a group of chairs assembled at Sunshine Booksellers on Marco Island for a reading and book signing featuring my favorite novelist, one who profoundly influenced my journey to becoming a writer. On the chair next to me was the latest book written by the featured artist, arguably the heir to John D. MacDonald, and two of my more popular short stories written under the byline, *Adventures of the Saltwater Cowboy*. I wasn't vying for more time, but more appropriately, an uninterrupted amount, as I had some things I wanted to say. First, I'm not the same person I was at the last book signing I attended many years ago. The big difference - I wasn't a published writer then.

Sitting at a fold-out table against the far wall, he looked more like a football coach or baseball skipper (coach) than a New York Times bestselling novelist. I noticed the mono-filament line tied around his glasses as a makeshift lanyard and realized he could even pass for a fishing guide.

I approached the table as the last fan walked away, grinning, admiring the personal note. Then, with an outstretched hand, I flashed my best movie-star smile and reintroduced myself: "Jed Edwards." I saw a glimmer of recollection in his eyes and hoped it was from all the book signings, not the copyright infringement notice.

It's not as bad as it sounds. In 2014 my stepbrother, Scott McLeod (R.I.P.), asked me to write a piece on the state of skateboarding from the viewpoint of an "aged skater" for his online magazine, *Deprived Society*. The theme manifested immediately, as a few weeks prior, my viewpoint was crystal clear as I was jettisoned from my skateboard by the force of a main tendon rupture – the Achilles.

The fact that the after-school teacher had been skating with my son and me could have contributed to the possibility that I may have been pushing my limits. Therefore, I ignored the tightness in my heel as I came around for the next run. I wanted to make sure I had enough speed going into the carve, and I gave two more full pushes. Then, "*BANG!*" some soccer mom on a crotch rocket sped up behind me and slammed me in the back of the legs with a two-by-four, at least that's what it felt like. Before becoming intimately familiar with the pavement of the parking lot of my son's elementary school, I registered that sound, like the "crack" from a 22-long rifle as my Achilles tendon snapping.

With parents still picking kids up in the car line, I laid in the gutter with my head resting on the curb, my left foot flat on the surface, and my right leg crossed over my knee to support my wrecked and dangling foot. I don't remember the pain as much as I do the trauma; more like a violent car crash than a sports injury. However, the humiliation as every mini-van, S.U.V., and alternate fuel truckster rode slowly by, asking if I needed assistance, would live in infamy in my brain. I didn't need an ambulance or an E.R. visit. I knew what had happened the moment I felt the tendon break and heard the sickening "pop" in my head. There was nothing anyone but a surgeon could do for me. Since it was Friday afternoon, I was on my own until Monday. If not for my legendary reflexes during critical times, as chronicled in many of my short stories, I would have assuredly suffered more significant injury from that wipeout, which had to have been spectacular.

Na," I waved them off, "I'm good, just catching my breath…. Happens all the time." The embarrassment faded when I realized that a gnarly wipeout resulting in a grisly injury must have made a hell of an impression on the after-school teacher. I lifted my head from the curb and looked around, but she was gone.

Remember, people, this was 2010 – I no longer have the option of skateboarding with child caregivers.

Back to the skateboard piece. Like many of my stories, I didn't know the title until well into the writing process. Then, *bang*, there it was. My perception of the event in relation to the world, six feet (one fathom) off the ground in flight, reminded me of a reference from my favorite author's flagship series. Because the title had nothing to do with the content, the thought of it being problematic never occurred to me.

The piece ended up being more than a short story. It was more an ode to the sport in the 80s when skateboarding was still a crime, when skaters accessed terrain by any means necessary, which, in some instances, could be defined as trespassing. The bonds formed by a group of skaters pushing each other's physical and mental limits in the face of danger and personal injury while sometimes skirting the boundaries of the law are unmatched in competitive sports. The competition was within us, not each other.

Tragically, Scott passed away before publishing the issue that would have featured my piece. When the shock of losing my brother subsided somewhat, I realized how proud I was of the story and posted it on my Facebook page, hoping somebody might read it.

Not long after, I received a "seriously fonted" direct message notifying me of a copyright infringement. I perused the notice enough to realize it was legitimate. A lot to take in, I leaned over and placed my head in my hands. I called a friend, trusted proofreader, and fellow fan of The Author and told him the news.

"Man… that's awesome."

"I know, right?" I couldn't believe it. He'd read my story and cared enough to call me out.

"What are you gonna do?"

I thought for a moment. "I'll change the name of the story, then craft a carefully written apology… problem solved." So, that's what I did.

Sometime later, I received his response, and my spirits drifted away like ash from a burned-out campfire. Only after consulting with his people did he understand. He said he didn't have a problem with it and that I could keep the name for my story. Dang… my heart sank. He didn't read it. I felt like beating up on myself like Chris Farley – idiot. I wanted to respond with, "Are you sure you don't want me to change it?" But I didn't, instead thanking him for his generosity.

Back in the present… I laid the two stories on the table in front of him, gambling with my pride that he hadn't made the connection. Finally, I said earnestly, "I'd like you to know that I hadn't written a sentence until I started reading your work."

He donned the reading glasses hanging from his neck and perused my short stories for seemingly long enough to get a feel for my "voice." When finished, he took his glasses off, looked at me, and said, "And now you're published."

I repeated his words to him, "And now I'm published." I held my head a little higher and added proudly, "The Coastal Breeze News AND the Everglades City Mullet Rapper."

I showed him some interesting mementos from over the years, including an article published eons ago after a book signing at the old Sunshine Booksellers location and a picture of six author-signed novels I dug out of an apartment fire in Las Colinas, Texas, in 2010. They're warped and stained from the smoke and water from the fire hoses – maybe even a little mildewed.

I looked at him and said, "When people say they're your biggest fan, they're not your biggest fan." The implication needed no explanation. Then he did something he didn't have to do; ask me to sign my stories to him, and he would put them in his office.

We talked about the 10,000 Islands and marine violations (mine, not his, as chronicled in more than one Adventure of the Saltwater Cowboy). Never once did he appear put out or disinterested. On the contrary, he gave me the impression that he could have carried on. However, I gracefully bowed out on a high note and bid my farewell. A second too long and the experience would have been sullied. Hopefully, this was his introduction to Jon Edward Edwards. That pain-in-the-ass copyright infringer was "Jed," anyway.

On the way out, I announced to the staff loud enough for anyone in the room to hear. "Y'all be looking for the latest Adventure of the Saltwater Cowboy. Comes out in the Breeze tomorrow." I walked to my truck more confident than ever with the swagger of an up-and-comer.

27

Hooked

The visibility improved as the sun bled through the eastern tree line, although I was still fishing blind. Through the fog, I heard the propellors on the topwater lure, a Devil's Horse, thrash the surface with each twitch of the rod tip. The air was calm and heavy, and the humidity felt like a fleece jacket. Sweat ran down my face stinging my eyes, yet I couldn't take my hands off the reel. Tucking my chin into my armpit, I dragged my face across my shirt sleeve. It was a fine late Spring morning in Southwest Florida to be rippin' lips. The bite had been fast and furious after arriving through a gap in the fence, traipsing through the palmetto and scrub brush, and picking off hundreds of those little "hitchhikers" that stick to your socks and shoes like tiny leeches.

Twitch, reel slack, *Twitch*… wait, *"BLEOW!"* He knocked it out of the fog and into sight, where it plopped. Letting it sit, I watched the water rings dissipate. Then, as predator fish do many times after striking, he struck again, the first hit not necessarily a "strike" but a "stun" to disable the prey. *Hooked up!* Shifting my weight from one side to the other, counteracting the fish's movements, and leading it away from obstructions along the bank, I did the "tight line dance." All the while looking over my shoulder like a thief in the night, as the area I was fishing may have been posted. Who can ever really tell about these things?

I pulled the healthy two- to three-pound Florida strain largemouth bass onto the water's edge and carefully "lipped" it with my non-dominant hand's thumb and index fingers while carefully working the hook(s) out with the other.

Anyone who has ever caught and released a fish caught on a lure with treble hooks knows this is where things can get interesting. There are six points, six barbs, and three per hook. Pliers are the proper tool. However, sometimes the situation calls to travel light, such as the possibility of an escape and evade; in 00Redneck training (James Bond has nothing on us), pliers are deemed non-essential in this type of mission. So you wing it and hope the fish will be still, but they don't always, in which case you may find yourself in quite the pickle. Which is what happened with one unexpected flail, one flip - I was hooked.

I imagine I resembled a looter carrying a 40-inch plasma after Katrina as I hiked back through the brush to my truck, holding my hand close to my body, hook, lure, line, rod, and myself one unit. If the barb wasn't sunk into the meat of my finger, it was by the time I opened the heavy bed cover of my truck and rummaged around in my toolbox, searching for a tool adequate to reduce the drag until I reached the walk-in clinic. During what felt to be about ten minutes, every move I made shook that Devil's Horse, and every time it did, I felt the hook digging around, twisting in my finger.

Some of you may be grimacing, imagining the trauma – sympathizing. Upon seeing my Facebook post, my cousin, Blair, texted me a video of himself performing the procedure on himself, complete with a moniker that means "less than masculine." Where I come from, you're probably not very popular if your friends don't haze you.

For someone to perform at a "world-class" level, they will have over 10,000 hours of deliberate practice invested. As a writer, I'm about 40% there. As an angler, although I can't claim to be "world-class," I surpassed the 10,000 hours milestone decades ago. All that time near sharp hooks, and this would be the first visit to the ER. Considering all the close calls and near misses, those are pretty good odds – the story of my life thus far.

Running trot lines in the Mississippi River, my brother Barney was snagged by a hook. We had baited a section and were moving to the next, the small outboard struggling to keep up with the current, when suddenly, our momentum had stalled due to the hook in Barney's tricep. As I watched in horror, Barney pulled enough slack in the trotline against the current to free the hook from his arm. That was some Huck Finn stuff right there.

Reggie and I were trout fishing in the grass flats of Gullivan Bay (when there used to be some) when he ended up with a #3 circle hook impaled in his finger. In the blink of an eye, Reggie grabbed some pliers and yanked that sumbitch out – just like that.

Ned "bapped" me upside the head at Black Bayou with a Texas-rigged bullet weight that had to feel close to being hit with a small lead sap. Or maybe I slapped Ned with the weight in my backcast. I'll have to ask him.

My coup de grace of close calls with treble hooks would be the two instances I had to take Turk to the emergency pet clinic. Turk was my Feist, who lived to be sixteen years old. I never went fishing without him, ever. He either loved fish or hated them because as soon as one hit the deck, Turk was on it. Once, he ended up with a rattle-trap in his paw, and the other time he attacked a bass that had yet to be released, resulting in bass, crank-bait, and dog joined as one. You can imagine how that went. After all that, fishing on the bank of a small inland pond did me in.

So, I go ducking in and around posted and no-trespassing signs and run down banks from security guards holding a rod with a fish attached to it? Which did not happen in this instance. Say I have an accident on your proper-ty? Believe me; I don't want you to know I was there. 00Redneck, remember? I'm addicted to the pull on the other end of the line, the anticipation and rush of the strike, the thrill of victory, and the agony of defeat.

Regardless of my debauchery, I will leave an area better than I found. I don't care if it's picking up one piece of trash. I realize that's not a feather in the cap of fixing the environment. It's just an example. It could justify my tomfoolery, "*I may steal your diamonds - I'll bring you back some gold.*"

As a generation X white man from Louisiana, I must be a rebel-rousing, animal killing, crude oil burning, assault rifle-toting, hell-raising, environment hater. I may be many of those things, but as a Saltwater Cowboy, the backwater is my sanctuary. I challenge anyone to match my passion for the environment.

The last animal I killed was a buck I'd hunted all season in 2008, but only because I moved from Texas and had a black Lab nearly the size of a South Florida whitetail, and I haven't killed an Osceola Turkey yet. Regarding assault rifles, I was thinking of getting one for the upcoming apocalypse. Otherwise, I have no use. However, my friend, Tiny, has several if I feel like firing off some rounds.

Any true sportsman is an environmentalist. Why people from other parts of the country don't understand this is beyond me. We're not all down here dumping cases of Ziplocs in the water.

28

───────

Ditch City

Growing up with an attractive mother can be traumatic. "Man, your mom is hot" evokes a different emotion than "Man, your girlfriend is hot." See that? Feel that? Not so lovely, is it? Truckers eyeballing as they sped by faster than an eighteen-wheeler should. I can't speak about what I overheard on the C.B. one day. Something no eleven-year-old kid should hear about his Mother. I'll go ahead and say that I don't remember what they said. At any other time, I would write what I thought they may have said and said I didn't. That's why my genre is "Creative Non-Fiction."

We moved across the Ouachita River to West Monroe when Mom and Ronnie split up circa 1982. I started third grade at yet another school, Highland Elementary. Mom taught fifth grade at our rival school, Claiborne, a few miles away. We had no money but went to Friar Tucks on Tuesday nights for fried chicken and fried biscuits. One night we met a guy who fixed our Volkswagen Rabbit for free. Therefore, in theory, it was kind of like marketing. Wednesday nights, we had Mc-Chicken's, which had just come out. I believe Johnny's Pizza was Thursday night.

Buck Night, the dollar matinee at East Gate Cinema in Monroe, was a thing of ours too. I can't remember which night it was. Apparently, we never knew because I recall driving by the theater one night in Mom's recently upgraded Mazda 626 to ask. Daph rolled down the window and asked a young Southern Gentleman taking long strides towards the box office, "Is this Buck Night?"

He stopped in his tracks, looked back, and replied with passion and fervor, in an accent all to itself, West Monroe, "Naw! This Bustin' Loose!" Referring, of course, to the 1982 comedy starring Richard Prior. That could be the funniest moment of my life thus far.

When returning to "Ditch City," our subdivision appropriately named for the exposed storm-drain system, we took evasive maneuvers to check our six and ensure we didn't have a tail. It wasn't uncommon for admirers (stalkers) to show up like that asshole in the Datsun 280Z, that dude that sent the cards daily, and that other guy. The property developer must not have had enough money in the budget for civil construction. The result was a series of concrete ditches approximately five or six feet deep and 10 to 15 feet wide. It didn't seem that strange then, the setting, not the stalkers, but looking back, especially as a construction professional, I realize how archaic it appeared—the perfect set location for a post-apocalyptic dystopian society thriller. A place stranger than fiction where being viciously attacked by crazed *Ditch Trolls* was a legitimate concern.

Now, those West Monroe boys play tough, and it didn't take long to find out where I stood on the "fight or flight" phenomenon. And because I come from a long line of fighters, Mom the fiercest of all, I was ready when the fifth grader infected with rage attacked me in Ditch Four, Quadrant Five, on the west end of Ditch City.

She was big and mean and had a crazed look of determination in her eyes. I had to assume I'd said something untoward that rubbed her wrong in the lunchroom or on the playground, perhaps. She ran into the ditch with a rebel yell and raised fists. Taking nasty scratches to the face, I pushed her off, planted my feet, and smashed her in the nose with a straight right hand. I felt the cartilage collapse under my fist and the wetness of her blood as it splattered the dirty concrete behind her. Hands clasped over her face, she turned and ran home with a different attitude and cadence than when she'd arrived.

I went home and told Mom what happened. As she's inspecting my face, there is a knock at the door. I follow 92 pounds of fighting fury to the door, where she opens it to face a mad mother, her mangled-faced daughter next to her. The Mother wasted no time and was full tilt from the get-go. "Your son this! Your son that! Look at my daughter's face! Blah blah blah!"

Calmly, Daph said, "Lady, your daughter attacked him. Look at his face. Chris saw it." Chris Spikes was my next-door neighbor, four years older, de facto big brother, and pseudo "babysitter." I might not have said anything to the *Ditch Troll* at all. Now that I think about it, thirty-nine or forty-two years later, Chris could have instigated the whole thing. He was laughing a little too much.

Mom's attempt at diplomacy a failure, The Mother said, "You'll be hearing from my lawyer!"

Holding the door open wider, presumably to prepare should the need to slam it in The Mother's face arise, in her customized 80's workout garb, white high-top Reeboks, Mom asked, "Who's your lawyer?"

Standing up straight and proud, she replied, "Robert Carbone."

As if she knew the answer, like a secretary, Mom said, "Come back in an hour, and he'll be here," and shut the door. The Mother and The Daughter returned a few minutes later with their tails between their legs, apologizing. The Mother said The Daughter told her the truth after they left.

The high-profile Monroe attorney was the last Ditch City Admirer, as a few months later, we loaded up the 626 and moved back across the river to North Monroe – swimming pools, fancy cars. Robert's son, Seth, and I were the same age with similar interests. My step-sister, Sarah, was older (Chris' age), pretty, popular, with a reputation for being kind of wild, all good for me – street cred for the new kid.

In the years to come, it became abundantly clear that Robert was the most feared attorney in Monroe. Not only was it the consensus around town, but shitty attorneys don't have backhoes run through their houses. Hack lawyers don't drive S500s with key gauges down the side. It wasn't until I met my father-in-law (ex-father-in-law), Ron Powell (R.I.P.), did I learn that Robert was the nemesis of a large portion of the golfers at Bayou Desaird Country Club, whose members made a lot of money and had a propensity for cheating on their wives.

An infamously positive figure at the Country Club for decades, and one of the finest men I've ever known, standing in his driveway, barefoot, wearing khaki shorts and a golf shirt, a sharp contrast of tan and white at his sock line, with his brand of Southern Arkansas twang, Ron asked me, "So, your stepdad is Carbone?"

"Yes, sir."

He thought for a moment, took a swig of Bud Light and a pull of his Backwoods cigar, and said, "Well, you cain't help it if ya Momma married an asshole (drawing out the word, pronouncing it icehole slowly)." I must clarify that he apologized years later after getting to know Robert. "Babe, I'm sorry I called Bobby an icehole," Ron said memorable things frequently, some funny, some profound. I miss him.

If you've never been through it, then it may be hard to understand, but to kids, stepparents have a place until their place is decided, which can take some time. That place is out of their spouse's and their spouse's child's business unless specifically asked otherwise. All of you who did not grow up with divorced parents but, for whatever reason, decided your kids should, listen up.

Stepparents don't know shit and need to shut up unless specifically spoken to. At least until everyone is comfortable - any child of divorced parents will tell you the same. I saw that not only was Robert a phenomenal lawyer but a good father and husband to Daph. It didn't take long for me to trust him.

Believe me when I say that not only did Robert not have to be discouraged from "getting in our business," but many times he had to be dragged in. Such as the time I set Ms. Bev's apartment on fire. Ms. Bev was Clement's Mom, and when it came to parties, well… Ms. Bev was cooler than everyone else. Therefore, her apartment was the venue for many a party. She was on a "date" the night one thing led to another, and I poured gasoline on a charcoal grill that someone had started on the porch, second floor, I might add. Why there was a milk jug full of gasoline on the apartment next door's doorstep is beyond me. Why someone started a grill is beyond me, we weren't cooking. Regardless, it was a bad decision.

A couple of hours later, when the fire department left, I ran the half-mile home to break the news. But not before falling off the other side of the six-foot wood fence I chose to climb, ostensibly a shortcut, landing in a sitting position, the event that I believe led to a herniated L5-S1. A salient point may be that, like all our parties, this party included imbibing in activities suited to an older crowd – copious amounts of booze.

We may be the only group in the history of modern society to feel the need to create false identification for drinking purposes when the drinking age was still

eighteen. Not to jump stories, but Robert is responsible
for shutting down our fake I.D. ring, which was on the
cusp of breaking out when he found the materials under
my bed in the Cabana. The "Cabana" was the pool house
and my room during high school. Amy and I were the
masterminds, she painted the backboard, and I figured
out the covering (a specific plastic had to be used). We
had tape on the floor to mark where to stand before the
backboard and everything. I had two aliases, Paul Andrews and Alex Lee. At the time, it was a buzzkill. Who
knows, maybe I had a future in that trade. But, in all like-
lihood, Robert kept me and my partner in crime, Amy,
from doing hard time.

        Back to the fire at Clement's, I got home feel-
ing punched in the butthole (L5-S1), woke Mom and
Robert, and told them what happened. Mom jumped up,
and we got in the Suburban and drove back to the scene.
Smoke was everywhere, the front door open, and we
could hear a commotion upstairs. A voice rang out in the
night, "Don't chu be no smartass!" It was Clement's battle cry. When he said it, someone was about to get their
ass whipped. I took off up the stairs the moment before I
heard the *Boom!* to find Clement and this dude Ms. Bev
went to an event with as a favor to Papa Flo (R.I.P.),
some so-called private investigator, crashed through the
drywall. Magnum Loser ended up in the better position,
and I ran to get involved. After all, Clement wasn't mad
at me for catching the apartment on fire; he was mad at

his Mom's date for being an asshole about it. I couldn't let that stand.

Mom jumped on my back, slowing my advance, giving Barney time to slip his finger into a belt loop in Private Numbnut's pants and pull Private Unlucky off of Clement. I'm flailing around trying to dump Mom on the couch; she's screaming, Ms. Bev is screaming, and Susan Florsheim is hitting Inspector "Don't mess with Clement" with a broom. He turned around and took a wild looping swing at Clement. Clement ducked and, with a nuclear warhead overhand left hand, dropped him. He hit his head on the coffee table and fell on the carpet bleeding, feet six inches off the floor like he was working his abs, his arms straight out, fists balled – "stiffed."

Upon returning home and telling Robert the story, he declares, "Am I going to be the only one in this family without a criminal record?" You see, I had already had a couple of brush-ins, as did my step-brother, Suntan Seth, and my step-sister, Sarah. She'd pulled a doozy and ran the Jimmy into Mrs. Jefferson's living room on Deborah Drive, just up from Norm Clausen's, my hit and run and victim. If not for his damn Cutlass getting in the way, Kevin Adams, and I could have slid right on through his yard, into Ned's, and back onto the street. Ole' Norm was standing at the counter at the Monroe Police Station filing a report when Robert brought me in after sobering me up, of course. This is another story in itself.

I won't get too deep into the third event of the Summer of 90' when I ran Robert's Master Craft into the train trestle on Bayou Desiard. I can see clearly in my mind Ryan in the rearview flashing "thumbs up" as I banked into a turn that no one in their right mind pulled a Hydroslider (kneeboard) through. I'll never forget when the shock of the collision subsided, my other brother in debauchery, Matt Freeman, leaning over the starboard bow inspecting the gash. Like a Redneck Spicoli, he said with Redman dripping from his "Booty Chin," "I can fix it." It was *Fast Times* in North Monroe. I worked all senior year at the Warehouse Restaurant washing dishes to pay Robert back for the insurance deductibles I racked up that Summer.

Every stepchild should have a "Robert" a figure as high on the family hierarchy as parents, someone you love and respect the same, just with a different dynamic. Will's Granddad, my consigliere and most trusted adviser, Robert, is not merely a sounding board for his wife like many stepfathers I know.

Mom, I've never thanked you for my "Robert" because it took writing this to understand. So, thank you. I don't tell you enough that I love you or give you enough credit. Without you, I wouldn't have made it this far in life, literally. Without you, you wouldn't be reading this, as I would never have discovered this talent I apparently have.

I'd like to think the chain of events after my fight with the fifth grader was serendipitous, leading to the best stepparent experience a kid could have. It could also be the origin story for the Saltwater Cowboy. The water in those ditches I played, and fist-fought in ends up in the Ouachita River, intersecting with the Mississippi and pouring into the Gulf of Mexico, where it doesn't get any saltier, Amigos.

29

Lake Claiborne Fire Drill

One cold winter's morning on a clear water reservoir in the piney woods of rural North Louisiana, Dad, Paw J, and I had caught a "mess" (a bunch) of white perch (North Louisiana speak for crappie). In the deep water near Lake Claiborne damn, bouncing jigs near the bottom, I remember my fingers stinging with cold when I had to take my gloves off. I must've been five or six years old. What happened at the end of the day is one of those things that stays with you forever.

Paw J was a tinkerer, you see? Some of his inventions were ingenious, but most weren't, such as the cage/trap-looking thing I'd noticed earlier in the boat. About one foot in diameter and a couple feet long, it came to a point at the end and had a trap door - a cage. But for what?

I remembered Ronnie asking Paw J about it, to which he mumbled something and changed the subject—another one of Paw J's contraptions…, always MacGyvering something.

Looking back, I'm pretty sure ole' Paw J was classic ADHD, which explains much of his "eccentric" behavior, like when he dropped Ronnie and me off at the dock; instead of tying up and getting out, he shoved off without saying a word. Dad started hollering, "Hey! Where the hell are you going!" Off Paw J went, that cylindrical cage-looking thing riding shotgun.

He stopped in the middle of the lake, got up, and started fiddling around, up and down, transferring this to that, tying stuff, hooking things up. Too far to see details, but whatever it was had given my dad what we call a case of the "red ass." At a steady pace, back and forth on the dock, cussing, "WTF is he doing? Is he putting all those white perch in…" Dad stopped in mid-sentence when Paw J threw the cage out of the boat, sat down, started the boat, and took off.

Ronnie had figured it out. In disbelief, he said, "He's trying to knock the scales off the fish…" Paw J's latest idea was to "scale" the fish without having to "scale" them. Why would one go to such lengths for such a thing? I've asked myself that same question. My only explanation is that a popular way of cooking white perch in Louisiana is to deep fry them whole, requiring the scaling process.

There they were, out there skipping and bouncing on the black water of Lake Claiborne like a flailing barefoot waterskier.

Paw J came back to the dock slower and less chipper than he'd left, ostensibly dreading what he was about to have to say. I imagine as he approached, he saw his son's mouth moving and knew he was being cussed. The cage was inside the boat, but as he got closer, we saw no fish.

Reaching the dock, in his "easy like Sunday morning" delivery, he said, "Ronnie, I reckon I might've lost them fish…" The latch on the cage door had come undone, allowing all the fish out. I don't remember how many – a "mess," like I said.

Amidst Ronnie's rant, one thing stood out. Red in the face, waving his hands, "GOING OFF WITH YOU IS LIKE BEING ON A CHINESE FIRE DRILL!"

All these years later, I wonder what happened to those fish. Crappie are a hardy species. *Can fish live without scales? Hmm...* I guess that depends on how well Paw J's contraption worked. Probably not too well, or someone would have patented the idea by now. Maybe a better explanation is the lack of demand. Only a full-blooded Redneck, a purebred, could have the motivation and wherewithal to design and build a mass fish scaling device. Let's face it: we're hardly a demographic large enough to market to.

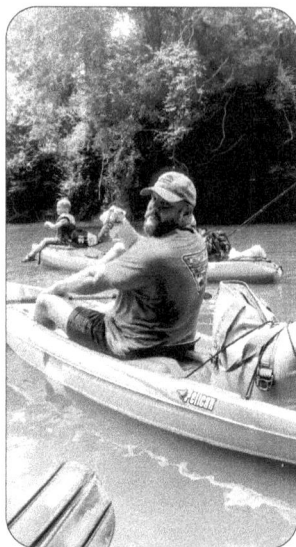

30

Past the First Bridge

Centuries-old live oaks canopied the waterway, opening a tunnel into different parts of the planet - rainforest, perhaps. Bend after bend; we paddled in the tea-stained current through the dense piney woods and bald cypress of Desoto National Forest.

"Man, this is just like I remember it," I told Jason Philips, my best friend during eighth and ninth grade. Jason is one of my Amigos who has always been and will always be an Amigo, as are a handful of other Mississippians.

"Ain't much changed around here," he said as he laid his beer between his legs and moved his paddle to avoid a fallen limb. The leaves of the branches were still green with life and bobbed in the current as we floated by.

I couldn't help but notice the massive biceps with every twelve-ounce curl Jason did. "Damn, Bubba," I said, "Where'd you get them arms?" He just laughed and did another rep while somewhere in the distance,

Hank Jr. sang;

I've got some fond memories of San Angelo
And I've seen some beauty queens in El Paso
But the best-lookin' women that I've ever seen
Have all been in Texas and all wearin' jeans

The feeling of being stuck in a time warp started when I paid $3.50 for a can of Copenhagen at the convenience store in New Augusta, which cost $9.00 in South Florida. "Three-fifty? For a can of snuff? Are you sure? It cost nine in Florida."

"You in Mississippi now, Baby," said the girl behind the counter. Too often, all I see in development are places I used to hunt and fish, among other outdoor endeavors. A place such as this, where the woods are thicker than you remember and the rivers and creeks just as wild, gives me hope for the planet.

My steadfast and unwavering quest to become a novelist led me to a backwoods creek worming 40 miles through the coastal plain of southern Mississippi. A sandbar downstream of an ancient train trellis is the site of a tragic event that leads to spectacular drama in the decades to come. I can smell the creosote in the timbers thinking about it. However, I'm not creative enough to make something out of nothing. I have to have a tether, something I can make real, then I can roll.

Black Creek, resembling a stretched-out Slinky on an overhead chart, is one of a handful my friends and I roamed when I lived in the area during my teens. I needed to go back. My son moving from Texas to South Florida for college provided the perfect opportunity.

I called Jason and asked him if he had time to take us to some of these locations on our way back to Marco Island. About an hour later, he called back and asked if we had time to kayak Black Creek. "Is that the place we camped on the sandbar by the trellis?"

"Yep."

"How long will it take?" I asked, even though I knew I'd make time. Opportunities like this, as a Sportsman, are hard to pass up. The only obstacle was a rendezvous with the Greco Twins in Bay St. Louis later that evening.

"About four 'aers." (four hours)

I ran the math and ciphered that we did have time. "Hell, Yes," I replied.

Natalie and Laurie Greco are among a hefty handful of people, including Jason, whose friendships have transcended time. I've been lucky that way. At first, people assume the "Twins" aren't twins, like it's a joke or nickname because they look nothing alike. Although equally stunning and magnetic, an exotic-looking brunette and a bombshell blond. Now and then comes a civilian, in this case, two, with such exceptional personalities that they become pseudo-regional celebrities.

The Twins were having a birthday party for my Mentor in Mayhem during college, Jimmy Bershen, at Laurie and her husband, Jonathan's, fishing camp on the coast – an hour-and-a-half drive from New Augusta.

Bershen and two other close friends, Staab and Chris Edwards, who I hadn't seen in decades, would be there. To top it off, the Twins weren't telling them I was coming.

Three hours plus of our estimated four-hour trip flew by. We'd passed the trellis and sandbar where, in my story, the teenagers were camping and the patch of woods where the two girls went missing. I figured we were nearing the end, and I thanked my friend again, as this experience is vital in my creative process.

"Don't mention it, man. I hope y'all make it to Bay St. Louis on time. Matter of fact, y'all may want to go ahead downriver. When I said the trip would take four hours, I didn't realize the current would be this slow. I didn't know they'd be taking so many breaks either," Jason said of his contingent of Golden Eagles (USM mascot).

They'd stepped up the shenanigans and were in rare form. Such as Michael riding a giant oak limb that was stuck in the sand, bobbing in the current, waving his hand like a bull rider. I don't know if telling them if something interesting happened I might make a story about it made a difference or not. Regardless, they didn't have to do anything, being themselves was enough. Like when Tommy fell out of his kayak attempting to catch a wayward beer thrown to him by Blake.

I heeded Jason's message and took directions to the landing where we'd staged our vehicles. "Simple," Blake said. "You'll see the bridge in the distance. When you do, hug the right side until you see the orange flagging - the landing. Can't miss it."

I should've known that it wasn't easy when Jason looked at me sternly and said, "Don't go past that 1st bridge, or you'll be in a bind."

It was 3:30 when Will and I said our goodbyes, shook hands, bro-bumped, and meandered down the creek. With one bar of service, I texted the Greco Twins and gave them an ETA of 5:30 PM - thirty minutes float time and a one-and-a-half-hour drive to Bay Saint Louis.

"This area is full of rich folklore and superstition," I told Will as we paddled on. The outlaw James Copeland was caught and hanged in New Augusta. His body was buried on the banks of the Leaf River, just across the way from here. The body was later stolen – or... perhaps disappeared." I was telling a version of what I remembered from ago.

"Disappeared?" asked Will. Now I had his attention.

"That's right. It's said that Copeland's ghost wanders the banks of the creeks, rivers, and streams around here looking for the treasure he buried."

"You're so full of it," Will said.

"The Dude abides. I'll tell you what…, I'd rather get lost in the 10,000 Islands than get lost out here. At night…, you've never seen pitch-black until nightfall."

The anticipated thirty minutes came and went. No bridge. *No big deal… it must be coming up.* Then, like a switch was thrown, the surroundings seemed different; the woods were fuller, and the pine trees were the tallest. I felt the current strengthen, and the water was clearer. Upon rounding the next bend, I saw why.

The west side was bordered by a thirty-foot bluff perforated with exposed root systems. On top sat a giant oak with a rope fixed high on a muscled limb. Young men in cut-off jeans swung out, letting go at the last minute, flipping or diving into the deep pool at the bottom. Which explained the increased current and cleaner water – a spring hole.

Next to the bluff was a landing alive with young glassy-eyed country folk, seemingly without a care in the world. Will and I stopped on the sandy beach and pulled our kayaks (borrowed from Tommy) onto the shore.

Initially, I misinterpreted their behavior as rude, as they glared at us. Not in a mean way, but more of a passive indifference. Especially when I asked if anyone had a phone charger we could use, they just laughed and carried on. "What the hell," Will said, "Do they even see us?"

"Doesn't appear that way," I replied.

Looking at his device, Will added, "I've got 18% battery."

"Let's hope it's enough," I replied as a pretty young lady with pink cheeks approached wearing a bikini and a baseball cap, oblivious or uncaring to the layers of flab protruding over the edges.

"Y'all lost?"

"Well, my friend told us the landing was before the first bridge. He said when the bridge comes into view, hug the right side of the bank and look for the orange flagging. But we've been paddling for two hours, and unless I blacked out and missed it, we never saw a bridge," I said in one long breath.

Later, I would beat myself up for being so blasé. Here we were, in the only body of water in Mississippi officially designated as a Wild and Scenic River. I took off like I'd gotten directions to the 7-Eleven I wasn't familiar with. The red flag the size of Texas should have been when Jason emphasized, "Do NOT go past that 1st Bridge. Or you'll be in a bind."

She smiled underneath a baseball cap and asked, "Sugar, what Bridge?"

As if I didn't understand the words coming out of her mouth, I said, "So you're saying there is no landing before the bridge...."

"I'm saying the only bridge over the creek is up at New Augusta. Somebody is messing with y'all," she replied. I knew that wasn't the case; it was a misunderstanding in the directions. We'd zigged instead of zagged somewhere. There had to be an explanation.

Minutes passed as we tried to reach Jason to no avail. The young lady was nice enough to offer us a ride on their way out. However, the last thing I wanted was to be looking for someone who was looking for me when I had no idea where I was. Therefore, we stayed put.

I became more uneasy as time passed. Not knowing where I am is unsettling. A prolonged sense of Deja Vu had begun to alter my perception, making it increasingly difficult to ascertain fantasy from reality. But when I saw the old outlaw wearing a duster dragging something up the bank, I knew for sure there was something strange about this ride. "What in the hell," I said, walking closer. Straining my eyes, I asked, "What's he dragging?"

Standing beside me, looking through the brush, Will responded, "Kayak?"

It wasn't a canoe or a kayak. It was something I hadn't seen in some time. "It's a pirogue," I said.

"A what?" Will asked, taking his face away from the bushes.

"A Coon Ass Canoe," I clarified.

"Oh," he said and resumed his position.

Dark hair, bushy black beard, weathered cowboy hat, dungarees of some kind, maybe tin cloth, tucked into beat-up cowboy boots, he moved quickly with the wide gait of a bull or bronc rider as he made his way to an old model Chevy Silverado that I hadn't noticed. The loud bay of a hound dog rang out, and a large animal with a short-spotted coat burst through a ticket and was headed our way – no doubt with bad intentions.

Will and I were about to run when the man said, "Wo now, Gus." The howling ceased as the dog hurried to its owner's side. It was a good thing because my cardio wasn't up for a "run for your life" "scenario.

Caked from head to toe in mud, we watched him drag the Cajun canoe past us, never looking at us or stopping what he was doing for a second. When he asked,

"You boys lost?" I looked around to see if there was any-one else he could be talking to.

"Uhh…, yes sir," Will said.

As he loaded the pirogue into the back of the Chevy, he asked if we wanted a ride. He said that there were only two places that we could be.

I thought about that for a moment… *"Only two places we could be,"* he'd said. *What the hell does that mean?* "How do you know where we're supposed to be?" I asked as we climbed into the truck. Me in front, Will and Gus in back.

"Because it's the only places you *can* be," he re-plied.

I felt like my nerves had been tasered. *What in God's green earth is he talking about?*

The entire ride Gus breathed his hot, rank breath on my neck; snarling when I made a move he deemed threatening. He had one mesmerizing blue eye – distinc-tive to a Catahoula Leopard Dog (or Cur), the state dog of Louisiana.

My heart dropped when the first place he took us to wasn't our landing. *He's taking us somewhere to kill us, dismember our bodies, feed us to Gus…* Rounding a dirt road veined with ruts my sense of direction returned, and I recognized the surroundings. There was the land-ing, Will's truck, and Jason and the Boys. The outlaw stopped in the middle of the road, we got out, and he left – that quickly. I didn't even have a chance to thank him.

"Goddamn! We were about to call the Sheriff." Jason said as we approached.

After telling the story, Jason, Tommy, and Blake busted out laughing. "What?" I asked, oblivious to what struck their funny bones.

"Dude, what truck? Y'all just came walking up the road there," Jason said.

Will and I looked in that direction, and I said, "I swear he let us out right there," pointing at the area we'd gotten out, at least where I thought we'd gotten out.

"Come on now," Tommy said. "Old Western clothes, pirogue… We all know the legend of James Copeland."

"I know about it, sure…, but what does it have to do with this? The guy was a creepy old cowboy dude who could be the Outlaw James Copeland for Halloween?"

"Ha!" Jason laughed. "You ain't changed a bit… crazier than ever."

I chuckled, unsure of what was happening, "Ha… right on." As an afterthought, I said, "Besides, I thought he was buried on the Leaf River."

Along with everybody else that reads Wikipedia," Michael said quite profoundly while everyone else yucked it up. Apparently, the lore was of greater detail among locals. Hence, why I'd never heard of such.

"The local legend is way more than what's on Wikipedia," Jason said.

Grabbing another beer out of an ice chest sitting on one of the kayaks, Tommy said," Next thing he's gonna say is he had a big ole' Catahoula Cur with him. Everyone laughed except Will and me.

It was around nine o'clock by the time we found the kayaks, reunited them with their owner, and drove to Bay St. Louis. The back yard was alive with spirits, and we could hear them when we got out of the truck. Tired and salty from the dried sweat, we walked under the camp, built twenty-feet high on round piling towards the noise.

Natalie and Laurie saw us first and met me for a big ole', three-way hug. Bershen's eyes got big, and Chris Edwards looked confused as if *they'd* seen a ghost. Pat Staab walked past me, nodded, and said, "What's up, dude?" Everyone laughed, including me, causing Staab to double-take. I saw the realization on his face. He grabbed me, said, "Comere, you sumbitch you," and bear hugged me.

"What the hell, Capt?" asked Laurie. (that's what they call me – pronounced without a "t") "Ya'll shoulda been here about four hours ago."

"Yeah," said Natalie. "Don't you think you could have at least called?"

"Y'all didn't get my text?" I asked.

They looked at their phones and, in harmony, said, "Nope,"

"Huh… Well, we had some difficulties," I said, Will and I sharing a careful glance.

The Greco Twins looked at me, like, *Well? Waiting…*

"Ya'll ain't gonna believe this..." In this case, the truth was better than any fiction I could have created.

If you remain open in heart and mind, you may find that the river of life will carry you down a tributary where things flow as they should. You can't see the path, but you can learn to read signs along the way, suggesting direction. Like traveling the backcountry, everything looks the same. However, if you know what to look for, the natural flow of water becomes more evident, such as life - where research for a novel flowed into another Adventure of the Saltwater Cowboy.

31

You've Been Documented

My life is riddled with odd juxtapositions, as those who follow the Adventures of the Saltwater Cowboy can attest. In a way, they make me who I am. A good ole' boy from Louisiana with a BS in Construction publishing <u>anything</u> "creative" is unorthodox. Regarding outward appearances, the "good ole' boy" standard would hold if not for the tattoos – I've lost count, thirty-something.

The latest example was transitioning from looking like a rockstar when my friend, Clement, flew me from Monroe to Love Field on Christmas Day – this was after learning Will, my twenty-year-old son, was to undergo emergency surgery the next morning – to a complete buffoon in the coming days through intermittently getting in trouble on the sprawling Children's Hospital of Texas campus.

Trouble, like many words in the English Language, is relative. A big deal to someone else isn't necessarily to me. Therefore, when my ex-wife (let's call her Donna) said, through tear-soaked, smokey blue eyes, "I got a call from security. You've been documented," I wasn't sure what she was talking about. For clarification purposes, they were tears of Mother's worry, not exacerbation or frustration via ex-husband abhorrence.

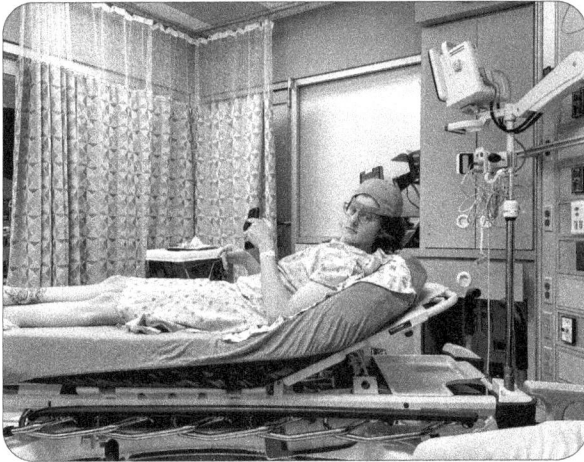

On day one of the scheduled endoscopic third ventriculostomy, December 26th, the Wizard of Hematology deemed Will's bloodwork "suspect" and sent him home with instructions to return for another blood test the following day. No one saw or talked directly to this entity, yet he, she, or it held the cards. The pediatric neurosurgeons didn't go until the Wizard said so.

I understood the problem to be a matter of viscosity, my knowledge being classified as ignorant. The aspirin he'd been taking for his headaches had made his blood too thin, not suitable for microscopic neurosurgery, or so they thought.

I volunteered to take Will back for the bloodwork as I hadn't had a chance to talk to him without the other people around since I'd arrived. My husband-in-law (let's call him Dwayne) was in my sight one hundred percent of the time, either glued to his wife's hip or lingering close behind, never letting the much younger Donna veer too far. Pleasing in a way, knowing that could never be me. A blessing I don't live with this woman who I thought was a partner in all things, but in reality, the real "not fake nice personality" was overbearing and manipulative.

It was the third day, the day after Will and I had gone for the additional bloodwork and the second attempt at surgery. The plan was to test his blood again, anticipating the numbers would continue to move in the right direction, as the previous tests indicated. When the medical team explained that the numbers went in the opposite direction and canceled the surgery for the second time, it was a tough pill to swallow.

I'd been with Will every day since he began having the headaches which had started weeks before. I knew how much he wanted it done, as did I. My emotional state, my ex-wife's anxiety, and Dwayne's permanent fixture status were more than I wanted to take. The sordid nature of her marital exodus and cruelty in the months to follow, combined with the lack of retribution, have made it impossible to find closure. Therefore, I excused myself.

Why, I'm not sure. Perhaps I didn't want to share that moment with someone less than a stranger, an interloper who helped strategize when and how to leave so that outward appearances suggested another marriage ruined by addiction while conveniently leaving out the mental diagnosis.

Why must I harbor ancient resentments that only serve to manifest new ones? Perhaps airing the grievance with a sledgehammer will purge me of these emotional toxins.

I'd only been gone about ten minutes, enough time to clear my head when I walked back into the pre-op room and was slapped in the face by a familiar but uneasy vibe; I'd done or was suspected of something.

There they all were: Will in the hospital bed waiting to be released, Donna, Dwayne, and my gracious host, Marsha, my ex-mother-in-law.

Being a "shoot first, ask questions later" kind of guy, coming under suspicion isn't unusual. My defense is subconsciously based on historical data that indicates the transgressions are, more times than not, partially my doing... exhibiting traits that can feint guilt. It's an uphill climb with a guilty affect out of the gate.

The first thing that came to mind was getting lost the day before and having to be escorted away from an area I had wandered into, like a dementia patient or someone up to no good, not just a dude with uber ADHD under immense stress. Not the generic variety of ADHD, but the diagnosed kind that causes a person to find themselves in restricted areas. Now..., I could've and would've found my way. I didn't realize I was lost until a security guard stopped me and asked, "Sir, are you lost?"

To which I had to answer, "Why, yes. I am." I was – lost. Me? I could've found my way; I wasn't concerned. I was writing something. Obviously, my faux pas was being a "wandering wayward old man."

I'm 50, by the way. I might be 51. The date on my birth certificate is "approximate," as I was dropped off on a doorstep. I'm just playing. Dr. Rahn Sherman delivered me. Bruised my eye pulling me out with tongs. He, Uncle Eddy, and Ronnie, my dad, had been out squirrel hunting. Doc Sherman gave Mom a twelve-gauge shell to bite. So, the story goes, and another one to tell.

"Crap… I was hoping not to have to talk about that," I said, blathering over being stressed, running on little sleep, juggling anxiety-laden moments like only one with reflexes such as I can. She said nothing. I continued, trying to explain away the lostness with a chart analogy "You told me to go to the same place we went yesterday. Which, if this campus could be laid out on map of the U.S., that would be Seattle," I pointed northwest. "But when we showed up, the hospital staff directed us elsewhere." I looked around to take the temperature of the room. Marsha seemed entertained, which was enough to stoke my confidence. "Before we knew it, we're in Miami," I turned around and pointed to the opposite corner.

I explained how I didn't want to subject Will to the long walk, leaving him comfortably in Miami while navigating to the Pacific Northwest, negotiating the perils of my stress-induced "hyper-mania" alone. "Hell," I said, "I ain't gone lie… I was looking at my phone and found myself down some corridor – lost. And you know how I do in a grocery store while talking on the phone," I said. She rolled her eyes in acknowledgment.

Standing there cross-armed like a "blond" Maggie Rhee from The Walking Dead in her form-fitting jeans and boots, looking at me like she liked me less than I already knew she did, she said, "What are you talking about?"

I thought of the next thing I'd done that could have offended someone. Because my instrument governing society's norms blew a fuse somewhere along the way, it took a minute. Motioning out of the pre-op room and down the corridor leading to the second-floor lobby, I blurted, "All I did was go down to the first floor and meditate on a bench."

More looks and no words confused me further. Taking a deep breath, I asked, "What are you talking about?"

Exhaling frustration, Donna said, "Something in the parking garage yesterday." The blue in her sweater accentuated her now clear eyes.

"Oh, that," I said, the memory rushing over. "That guy was an a-hole. Now, that was justified," I spoke with confidence.

It involved an anti-social parking garage attendant on the first morning. I don't consider myself the end-all-be-all when it comes to social graces. My reactions are generally involuntary. It's simple: when disrespected, a mechanism is triggered in my brain, releasing the chemicals responsible for aggression. I don't remember what I said, but the chicken s%# went and told the principal.

Donna said they told her these types of things must be "documented." Considering the altercation happened on the street and not the parking garage itself, the event probably wasn't captured on camera – prompting the call. I knew that was horse s#t. Parking Garage Guy was "butt hurt" over being called out. I don't care about perceptions; my conscience was clear.

My explanation and theatrics seeming to have appeased the sit'chation, I walked with them to their car to see Will off. My nature becoming affable again, Dwayne asked me where I was parked. Filson briefcase strapped to my back, Dunkin' Donuts bags falling on the concrete; I looked around and replied, "I don't know." Appealing to the professional engineer in Dwayne, I visualized the property in plain view and asked him where we were located directionally.

"South," he replied. Texas, for the non-geography challenged, thousands of miles closer to Miami than Seattle.

I orientated myself, turned 180°, and pointed north. "That way, but right now," I said, "I'm going where he's going," nodding to my son. "I'll worry about where I need to be when I get there."

Dwayne looked at me in a way that suggested bewilderment over a life lived so carefree, prompting my unsolicited response. "I go where the road takes me, Partner."

Arriving at their alternative fuel truckster, I bid everyone adieu and made my way back to Seattle and on to the next *Adventure of the Saltwater Cowboy.*

I would be remiss not to give credit to Will for his champion's attitude throughout the long and arduous process. I found comfort from my stress and anxiety time and time again by Will's coolness. The only thing that troubled him was the area of his head they would have to shave, which, unfortunately, was significant.

This story not only marks Will's health bill clean but signifies the continuation of a bright future for a sharp and handsome young man. I'm proud of him. With nothing holding him back, he's charging harder than ever. Well done, Lad. Well done, indeed.

Beautiful Day

A fishing guide with a clandestine past is forced to confront a long ago tragedy and stop an escaped death row inmate from exacting revenge on himself and others. **Beautiful Day** follows **Captain Max Dean** from his home in Marco Island, Florida, to the swamps of Southern Mississippi in this tale of adventure on and off the high seas.

Beautiful
Day

1

Black Creek

Goodland, Florida
New Year's Eve, 2013

New Year's brought the remnants of a Nor'easter that fed across the Canadian Prairies, sending record lows down the Eastern seaboard. By the time it reached Marco Island, it was a frigid fifty-seven degrees. Gusting winds had chopped Florida Bay into banging wave sets that herniate lumbar discs. From the top deck of my houseboat, moored at Caloosa Island Marina in Goodland, Florida, Palm Bay looked like a White Russian – heavy on the Kahlua, brown with foamy white caps.

I took a sip of coffee that damn near scalded my tongue. *Dadgummit...* Turk, my aging but ever-spritely rat terrier, and Vladimir, the obese and assertive grey tabby, had been topside before dawn. The unlikely pair have a habit of catching sunrise from the top deck, weather permitting.

My animals slept through the muffled voices and carryings-on of the guides who operated out of the marina, their tones giddy like schoolchildren in Dallas during a snow/ice day, as all charters were canceled. Down at Coon Key Pass, I could see the boats take off at the end of the no-wake zone and roll and bang into rough seas. I felt bad for Brook, the new eco-tour guide; too windy to fish but not to watch dolphins and hunt shells.

Supervising tourists requires a disposition that I don't possess. I know this because of my stop at the Louisiana Purchase Gardens and Zoo in Monroe, Louisiana, as the Captain of the Bayou Tour Party Barge along my journey to becoming a Waterman.

Shadows hid distant mangrove islands, and the morning sun cast copper strips through gaps in the overcast horizon. I thought how cool it would be if Travis McGee and Meyer were over there in Fort Lauderdale aboard the *"Busted Flush"* enjoying hot caffeinated beverages. In a parallel universe, maybe.

I took a tiny sip of coffee this time and pondered the conversation Emily, my ex-girlfriend, and I had the night before. I was surprised she'd called, her second husband having issued that moratorium on anything Capt Max Dean four years ago. I didn't blame him. I wouldn't want my wife or girlfriend associating with me either.

I recall the sweetness of her kiss and the way she giggled and squirmed and pulled away, but not really, when my lips got near her port side earlobe. Some images are forever imprinted – a thin sliver of what had been a mini skirt bunched around her waist like a belly chain. Palms pressed into my obliques like they were the pressure points for CPR while the rest of her moved to a beat and rhythm unto itself, one that she made ours. Those spots are now marked with twin black and red nautical stars. Maybe in the back of my mind, they're her handprints.

The feeling of her five-foot-three, one-hundred-and-five-pound body collapsing on top of me during what ended up being our last rendezvous, the words she spoke into my ear, and how she said them, haunt me to this day.

I often wonder what life would be like had Emily or I made a different choice and our fates combined. Becoming wrapped up in intangible things can be dangerous in my work. Not fishing or football, but my lesser-known occupation – paramilitary operator, where nothing is left to chance, no second guessing or half measures. Therefore, I ponder these things, but I do so without regret.

Oblivious, an orbital cycle spawned by an event horizon in a faraway galaxy was pulling us toward one another once again. This time, we would pass closer than ever.

I surmise Emily's husband temporarily suspended the moratorium because the subject matter wasn't to reminisce. This was no disgruntled wife's, wine-induced, reach out to an old flame amidst marital woes. It was related to a traumatic, although cathartic, event that I rarely discuss with anyone. Some would say it is the catalyst for my clandestine nature.

On a dark winter night deep in the bald cypress and towering pines of Desoto National Forest in Southern Mississippi, I discovered I was capable of taking a man's life. I didn't. It wasn't because I wasn't trying to.

Donnie Williams, an uneducated but cunning, back-woods river rat, who despite his chiseled-chin handsomeness, exceptional athleticism, and most likely the product of inbreeding, had abducted two of my friends, Jennifer and Amy, and was in the process of raping Jennifer when I tracked them down. My friends and I stopped him, but after a horrific fight, he got away.

The Mississippi State Police picked him up a few weeks later under suspicion of murdering a woman who was taken similarly and in the same vicinity as my friends months before. Yet, there was no one to save her.

The evidence was solid; however, the lack of material witnesses prompted the DA to call the eight of us to the stand to give our account of our interaction with Donnie. Our testimony resulted in a conviction. *Death Row Motherfucker.*

Emily had called to tell me that Jennifer was killed the previous night in her home near Greenville, Mississippi. The interesting part is that the night before, the eight of us, Jennifer included, had been notified by the US Marshall's Service that Donnie Williams had escaped from the Mississippi State Penitentiary in Parchman, a prison notorious for being impossible to escape given its open and sprawling nature - there is nowhere to go. Only unless someone were desperate enough and had the skills to reach the river would they have a chance to evade.

Greenville, where Jennifer lived, is just downriver from Parchman.

Spring - 1991
Rural Southern Mississippi

Southern Mississippi is beautiful and wild, much of it unmolested – the polar opposite of coastal Florida. Cut with little rivers, streams, and creeks lined with bald cypress and bordered with tall bluffs, it's one of the best-kept secrets in the South – a teenager's Nirvana.

Black Creek, the only river designated by the state as "Wild and Scenic," worming forty miles through the coastal plain, is where my friends and I were camping that fateful night.

Winter was upon us, and although the first cold snap of the year hadn't hit, it was chilly enough to need a fire, a jacket, and a tent with a warm body to share it with. At that time, if I had a choice of who to share a confined space with and huddle for warmth with, it would have been Emily.

Football season was over now, and for the last several weeks, despite rebuke from coaches and family, I'd spent most of my time skateboarding with Team Beautiful Day. Paul, Alex, Miller, and I were the newest and youngest of the team. With legitimate ties to Tony Alva, to me, it was cooler than being the starting quarterback. Which I wasn't yet.

We'd set up camp on a large sandbar adjacent to an old railroad trestle. Four canoes beached, four tents pitched, one fire burning, eight souls laughing and carrying on without a care.

The girls weren't matching us beer to beer, but they weren't teetotaling either, venturing into the woods periodically to do their business.

When someone noticed Jennifer and Amy had been gone longer than they should have, the guys and I took our flashlights and headed into the dark of night—woods as thick as anything you could imagine, some pine trees twenty inches in diameter. If someone kidnapped you, slapped a burlap sack over your head, and dumped you out there, telling you it was South America, you would have no reason to doubt them.

We walked through the first patch of woods, hollering their names, up the bluff to the train tracks, and down the other side to a black wilderness. After an exhausting search, our spirits were low when a flash of light came out of a sea of darkness as if someone needed a flicker for reference.

I worked my way through the lush vegetation in the direction I saw the light until I reached the edge of a clearing where I stood and let my eyes adjust to the darkness. Through a break in the clouds, three trailers came into view. Thirty-foot double-wides strapped to cinderblocks arranged in a U-shaped pattern with a deck joining them in the front.

It hadn't occurred to me until that point that I was alone. I must've lost the others in the darkness. I shoved the thought from my mind. Out of the three, I had no idea which one the light came from. I crept to the first trailer and duck-walked along the side with my arms spread eagle on the surface, feeling and listening. I reached the end, jaked the corner, and went up the other side. Nothing… Running for the second trailer, I saw it wobble on its foundation and heard mumbled voices from inside.

I ran around the front and up the steps as light as a feather, making every effort not to telegraph my presence. I leaned in. I heard a girl's muffled cries. Turning around, facing away from the door, I lifted my right knee, and donkey kicked it, splitting the mechanism from the jamb. I ran in, Mag-Lite trained in the direction I'd heard the voices. There they were. Donnie Williams on top of Jennifer, Amy bound and gagged in the corner.

The space was empty, the floor caked with mud and pocketed with holes. The dank smell of mold permeated the air.

I only got a look for a fraction of a second, but it was enough to see that Jennifer's face was a battered mess. I dropped the flashlight and sprinted towards them in the dark by memory, delivering a hit on Donnie that Ronnie Lott, legendary defensive back for the 49ers, would've been proud of. The blow was solid; he made a low guttural noise, and I felt his body go limp.

The four of us lay in the quiet darkness for what seemed like an eternity, although it couldn't have been more than two seconds. Moonlight peeked through one of the windows, illuminating Donnie's silhouette. He stood up and pulled his jeans from around his ankles, covering his bare ass. At that moment, I wanted nothing more than to end his life.

Then he reached for something on the outside of his right leg. My eyes had begun to adjust to the darkness, and in the dim glare, I saw him smile. He stood in a wrestler's stance - left foot forward, holding a boot knife. In that instant, an eerie calm set over me. I wasn't scared. On the contrary, I was looking forward to punishing him.

I'd picked up the Mag-Lite and was shining it in his eyes. Blindly, he came at me. Everything following is out of focus, like a dream that I only remember bits and pieces of, like dropping the light and diving to the left. Why, I don't know, an atavistic response to danger, I suppose.

He caught me across the chest with what I later learned was a Buck skinning knife. It was the first, but not the last, time my reflexes saved my life - pulling away not unlike a boxer avoiding a right cross. More glancing than deep, the cut left a scar that makes the injury look worse than it is: flat, about half an inch wide and goes from my right pec to my left oblique. Although now it is well hidden amidst a sea of ink.

Donnie expected me to be in the direction I had dove. But when I landed, I crawled or scooted to the other side of the trailer. I stood up behind him and watched as he slashed and stabbed at nothing. I kicked him in the side of the knee as hard as I could. I heard it *"Pop"* as he dropped.

I'll never forget the noise he made; the femininity of his "shriek" was an eerie juxtaposition to the person I was fighting for my life. *"Ooh... Oweechee...,"* he lay there holding his knee like a scared child.

I ran to Jennifer, untied her, and was moving to Amy when Donnie got his wits back. I knew because Jennifer started screaming. I looked up as he was advancing with a raised knife - back to the evil agent from hell I'd been dealing with a moment before.

I would learn later in life that defending against a knife attack is the most terrifying type of hand-to-hand combat. There are no winners. I dodged his first stab, catching his wrists when he attempted a backhand slash. I could feel the cuts open on my hands and fingers and hear the blood splatter on the wall with each struggling movement for the blade. One of the girls shrieked, drawing Donnie's attention. I elbowed him in the face, causing him to drop the knife.

We scrambled for it; I snatched it up quicker and jumped on his back. I don't remember thinking anything but the most grievous thoughts you can imagine. I didn't want just to kill him; I wanted to hurt him first. I grabbed a handful of his hair in my left hand and hit him in the side of the head with the butt of the knife. I was reaching around to cut his throat when I heard my backup outside, as did Donnie.

I lost focus, and when he bucked, it threw me off balance onto the floor. I managed to get up before he pounced on me, but he grabbed my hands, and we fought for the knife once again. I remember thinking: *This is it, Max. Better Cowboy up now or take a dirt nap.* I prepared to give one last yank, everything I had, to try and pull my hands free without giving up the blade. Donnie anticipated my movement, and as I began the motion, he used my momentum to pick me up and sling me through the door. I dropped the knife and heard it clamor to the floor before the impact.

I crashed into Paul and Alex as they were about to enter. We fell off the deck trying to escape when Donnie emerged. Enraged, he bound down the steps, and as I scrambled to avoid him, I saw Miller standing at the tree line holding a limb. Paul also saw him, and in our effort not to telegraph Miller's presence, we did just that.

Miller was in his backswing when Donnie turned around and caught the limb under his arm. Dropping it, he yanked Miller close. Paul and I were paralyzed as Donnie clamped one hand around Miller's neck and held him still while reaching down and removing the boot knife. I remember being shocked that he'd retrieved it during the melee. Donnie was a unique individual.

Out of options and operating on instinct, I moved toward them with no semblance of a plan, my hands throbbing from the cuts when a crazed rebel yell rang out from the porch. A bloody Amy ran down the steps with raised fists, "Motherfucker! Piece of shit!"

Donnie turned toward her, holding Miller tight so they pivoted as one unit. She stopped mid-stride. Feeding off Amy's hatred, he smiled and pressed the blade harder into Miller's throat.

Alex, absent until this point, had found a sturdier limb and flanked the inbred psychopath. A tiny bead of blood had formed around the steel and skin of Miller's neck when Alex waylaid him, *"Crack!"* The limb snapped in two, and Donnie dropped like a sack of potatoes. As did Miller.

Jennifer had come outside, and she and Amy were sitting in a heap in the dirt, holding each other, crying. We ran to Miller, expecting him dead, but Alex's timing was perfect. The cut was superficial, like the one on my chest. The difference was fractions of a second.

The severity of the trauma had yet to resonate. I remember a feeling of euphoria that I would later compare to an opiate buzz. There was no absence of fear. On the contrary, my fear was sharp and constant. I was aware of every prick, but it did not consume me. I used it as fuel.

A few minutes seemed like an eternity, and time stood still. Everyone was as quiet, real quiet. Donnie's baby face and the moronic grin stuck on it came in and out of view as the clouds crept along in the starlit night.

Paul broke the silence. "Max, we need to hogtie this sumbitch before he wakes up," and pulled his belt out of his jeans with a *snap.* Alex approached with a handful of thick vines he'd pulled from a thicket to use for lashes and plopped them down.

Amy and Jennifer collected themselves and were tending to Miller while we, despite our mature performances until that point, groveled over the proper way to hogtie someone.

Out of a lifetime of surreal events, what happened next is at the top of the list. As we bent down to begin our hogtie, Donnie popped up. Almost knocking me down, he scrambled backward like a crab until he was several arm-lengths away. The light of the moon illuminated the dust that floated around his ankles, and I noticed his jeans were several sizes too short, barely touching the top of his boots.

He kept shinnying away, closer to the far edge of the clearing and deeper into the forest – never taking his eyes off us. Alex, Paul, and I looked at each other. I saw the concern on their faces as their eyes moved to my shirt, ripped and caked with crimson, and my hands, wrapped with shirt strips. "I'll be fine," I said, motioning towards our assailant, ever creeping away.

With a unified nod, we sprinted towards him. He ran faster backward, swinging his arms and pumping his legs like a defensive back on deep coverage. I'll never forget the look on his face as he held his middle finger on each hand up before disappearing into the brush, like a third-grade sore loser who took his ball and went home.

Our pace slowed at the tree line, unsure what was on the other side. *The crazy bastard could have stopped short and was in there, poised to strike.* "Hold up," I said, sticking my body half through the thicket and shining my flashlight, batteries nearly dead. "I think he's gone," I said and walked through.

A short patch of woods opened up to another bluff we didn't see until we nearly walked off it. We looked over the edge, but our lights were too dim. However, when we listened closely, we could hear the water. Paul dropped a rock… *splash.*

"Holy shit," said Alex. "Motherfucker Tarzaned right off of here in the black of fucking night."

As the three of us peered over the edge at nothing, Paul said, "Man, this is messed up. Let's get the fuck out of here. We're liable to run into Copeland's Ghost. Like this fucker (Donnie) ain't bad enough."

Paul referred to the legend of the Outlaw James Copeland, who was hung in New Augusta. The legend is that his ghost wanders the wilderness, searching the banks of the Leaf River and its tributaries for the gold he buried – a tale we all enjoyed around the campfires.

Back at the clearing and wondering what to do next, out of the darkness came a loud rustling. My primal instinct was that more danger was upon us. As I searched for a weapon, I heard Emily holler, "Max!"

The next voice was Jane Clair, "Miller!"

"Over here!" Alex yelled back as Emily, Jane Clair, and two middle-aged men they'd flagged down on the road two miles opposite our camp appeared. It was good they had found us, as my sliced chest and hands had begun to bleed worse after the sprint. I was in desperate need of medical attention, as was Jennifer.

I could see the horror on Emily's face as she ran to me, the blood-covered shirt and lacerated hands. She wrapped her arms around me, held me tight, and buried her face in my neck. Her tears felt cool on my skin, and her heart pounded against mine. And if I could have held her, I would have never let her go.

2

Caloosa Island Marina

I returned to reality when Turk took off down the ramp to the floating dock, sprinted to the end, and leaped into the water. Vladimir and I hustled to the aft edge and looked over the rail. There were no dolphins that I could see. Then, through the muddy water, I saw the huge dark shadow that Turk was following. "Vlad, he's chasing manatees now."

Communicating with me through the infliction of "meows," Vlad said, "Meow…," as if to say, *"Oh, dear."*

The previous night, I'd left a voice mail for an old teammate at the University of Florida, Toby Guillory, a Deputy US Marshal out of Dallas. The call we received was from a representative of the Marshals. However, it was brief and full of generic jargon - no information other than the inmate, Donnie Williams, had escaped and, per some Federal Statute, they (the US Marshal's Service) were required to inform those involved in his conviction. I had questions, and that was before becoming aware of Jennifer's demise.

I'd told Emily that Jennifer's death and Donnie's escaping was a coincidence, and the Marshals would catch Donnie soon. However, my intuition had been tested time and time again. If Donnie made it to the Mississippi River, depending on the river's stage and where exactly Jennifer lived in proximity to it – it's a foregone conclusion in my mind that he killed her.

The method of escape and the details surrounding it will confirm or deny the voice whispering in my ear. Toby would have specific information about both Donnie's escape and Jennifer's murder.

I climbed down, went inside, pulled an old Atlas from under a stack of charts and manuals, laid it on the table, and turned to the State of Mississippi. I laid the atlas down on the galley table and, with a red lead pencil, drew a circle around Parchman and one around Greenville and stepped back to think. Vladimir had waddled to the kitchen sink and was standing at attention. I waited for it… "Meow."

"Vladimir, I'm not lifting your fat ass onto the sink. If you can't jump, that's on you." There's an odd phenomenon with cats and running water – they like to drink from the tap.

"Meow?"

"Exactly."

Some find mine and Vlad's dialogue strange. They wouldn't be wrong; I've had an inexplicable connection with animals since I was a young sprite.

The last I'd heard, Amy lived in Natchez or maybe Vicksburg. I circled both. Jane-Clair, Paul, and Alex never left Hattiesburg. I moved my hand southwest and stopped. *Hmm...* Hattiesburg was a good jump from the river. I circled it anyway.

I couldn't remember where Miller lived, Baton Rouge, maybe. I marked it and Gulfport for Emily. With an architect's scale, I connected them north to south, leaving out the much farther southwest, Hattiesburg. In order: Jennifer, Miller, then Emily. Alex, Paul, and Jane Clair would require a risky jaunt somewhere in between. I took a deep breath and tossed the red lead onto the atlas. "Vladimir?"

"Meow…"

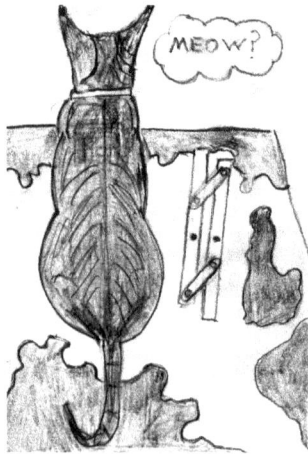

"Yep, I was thinking the same thing. We won't know jack until Toby calls."

It was still early in Dallas, and it being New Year's Eve, it could be a while before I heard from my friend. Therefore, I decided to get my workout in. I'd have my phone, an unfortunate appendage, if he called.

It was going to be a busy day, as my uncle, Larue, the proprietor of the marina, threw a New Year's Eve party every year. My job was to boil the live crawfish my buddy, Heath Clement, had flown in the day before. Still a little early for mudbugs, he'd gotten hold of one of the first batches of the season.

Somebody should pick up in here, I thought, walking around my houseboat, looking for particular articles of clothing. I found my jockstrap, running shorts, and a matching pair of socks that weren't too stiff. I dressed and stepped into my New Balance 990s, the best running shoes in the world, made in the USA. Grabbing my earbuds off the workbench (galley table), I exited the sliding glass door onto the rear deck.

The sun had broken through the haze, and it was lovely at sixty-two degrees, like the first spring day after a brutal winter somewhere else in the country. Spending most of my time outdoors, I wear the humidity of Marco Island like a wet blanket except for these three or four months a year, the time referred to as "season."

Turk was waiting in Golf Cart # 1 when I got in and stomped the accelerator. He shifted his weight forward in anticipation as the parking brake released with a loud *snap.* We wobbled down one hundred feet of concrete floating dock that felt as stable as a rope bridge over a Congo gorge.

Eight feet wide, one foot off the water, and no rails, it was nothing for me to lose a mode of transportation, whether it be a golf cart, skateboard, pallet jack, one of those things you use in Home Depot to roll plywood and drywall in. Hence, my "fleet" of third-hand beat-up golf carts. One day, when a tsunami sucks the tide out of

the bay, before the surge, it's going to look like a junk-
yard out here. The question is whether there will be anybody left to complain.

Coming to the end of the floating dock, we got
out, went up a gangway, and through a gate onto a fixed
pier, where we transferred to Golf Cart #2. Hegar, resident guide, and fellow live-aboard, was outside his
Trawler hosing down his bay-boat. I eased to a stop and
honked the horn. Jumping out of his skin, he tossed the
water hose where it landed on the handle, pointing dead
center of his face. "Goddamn it, Capt!" he hollered as
he yanked on the hose, taking the pressure off. "Jesus H
Christ, you scared the shit out of me."

I was laughing so hard I could barely get out the
words, "I'm sorry, bro…"

Once he got his composure, Hegar asked, "When
are y'all doing another show in the 10,000 Islands?" He
was talking about the TV show I did with a popular offshore guide out of Fort Myers, Jeb Copeland - *Adventures of the Saltwater Cowboys.*

"It'll be a while," I told him. "The next one is
out of Cocodrie, Louisiana, in February. Hell, it won't
be until April when the permit show up on the nearshore
wrecks." I use as many local guides as possible when I
do a show from home base, giving them some exposure.
Hegar had gotten some airtime and a credit on our show
out of Chokoloskee. The result was an increase in his
book (schedule of trips).

"Keep me in mind," I heard him say over the
"thumpity-thump" cacophony of tires racing over hardwood deck boards. I cut through a gap in the mangrove
peninsula that separated the boat slips from the marina

proper and followed the boardwalk to the parking lot, skidding to the side of the Shipp's Store with a stomp of the brakes. I got out, pushed play on my earbuds, and jogged down the long driveway to the entrance gate on Goodland Drive.

See it all around you… good lovin' gone bad

And usually it's too late when you… realize what you had

My mind goes back to a girl I met some time ago who told me…

Jogging through the tiny fishing village built on forty acres of ancient Caloosa Indian shell mound is like slipping through a tear in the space-time continuum and landing in the 1980s. As I ran, I tried to wrap my head around the logistics associated with escaping from a maximum-security prison. I decided that for a backwoods river rat like Donnie, Parchman would be the prison of choice to attempt an escape. Just miles to the Mississippi River, with Donnie's survival skills, he may never be seen again; he could live out his days like Huck Finn. However, that wasn't Donnie. His motivation was revenge, and he'd already started exacting it.

Structuring my cardio workouts around songs, I leave the playlist on "shuffle," giving the intensity a randomness. The song changed as I rounded the corner at Stan's Idle Hour and picked up the pace to the public boat ramp. My legs burned, and my bum knee throbbed as my nose siphoned every bit of oxygen from the even breaths it had to work with.

Pumped with fluid, inside your brain

Pressure in your skull begins pushing through your eyes

Burning flesh, drips away
Test of heat burns your skin
Your mind starts to boil

He could have floated away initially, but I don't care how able-bodied and clever a person is; traveling the Mighty Mississippi River with nothing but the clothes on your body would be one hell of a feat. He would have had to commandeer a craft to make considerable progress. Considering the types of vessels that abound on the Mississippi River aren't small craft, the only thing Donnie had experience with, this could've proven difficult.

After the sixth song, I stopped at Margood Harbor Park to stretch before returning to the marina. Larue, forty-eight, former All-Pro tight-end for the Colts, and Brook, the new eco-tour guide, threw a football around the lawn when I came jogging in. Larue put a thirty-yard effort into a twenty-yard pass that stung my hands - that quick, sharp pain that makes you want to bite nails.

Two fishermen began walking up the steep stairs to the ship's store. Larue trotted toward them, looking over his shoulder. I took two steps back, planted my feet, and threw a bomb that hit him in the hands at the stairway like an out-of-bounds marker. He caught the ball, dropped it celebratory behind his back, and ran up the steps as the marina collective erupted, *"Woohoo!!!"*

Brook had a climber's body with deep blue eyes and brown hair sun-kissed on the ends – a brunette. The last fact is remarkable for reasons that aren't relevant other than my houseboat, named "Occasional Brunette." It was a prank by my sophomoric friends while I was away, hinting at my unhealthy propensity for blonds. Saying it didn't play into my vanity and stroke my ego might be slightly untrue, and I, thus, kept the name. Besides, it's bad luck to change the name of a boat.

I was still shaking the sting from my hands when she flashed a precious crooked smile and said, "Captain Max Dean, International Man of Mystery." Her accent I associated with the mid-south, Tennessee, Kentucky, or West Virginia. "I didn't know you were a football player too."

"Well, that's because…, how old are you?"

"Twenty-seven."

"There you go. You were ten when I played my last game." I thought momentarily, then added, "Which would have been the 97' SEC Championship."

"I know, that's what I've heard. I thought you were just a fishing guide on TV who chases terrorists on the side."

The younger generations know me less for my TV show and less for being a football player. Most teens became aware of me after eyewitnesses placed me at the scene directly following the terrorist attack on the Horizon of the Deep oil platform in the Gulf of Mexico in May of 2010.

Some have said that I'm the government's personal spy. I can neither confirm nor deny those accusations. As far as being on the scene after the attack, people survived; I pulled many of them out of the water, oil still burning on the surface in places. People saw me and talked to me.

But I could deny everything else, *"Spy? Pppfff… Just happened to be in the area."* More complicated to explain was why my pilot buddy, Heath Clement (the one with the crawfish), and my brother-in-law, Ned, received Congressional Medals of Honor, and I didn't. The topic is a story in itself.

"Don't believe everything you see on the news," I said.

"I'm talking about what people say around here."

"Oh. Well…," my uncle saved me as I fumbled for words. From the walk-around deck of the Shipp's Store, in the most resounding booming voice you've ever heard. "Boy, when's Clement gone be over here with them mudbugs?" My uncle was talking about the live crawfish Clement professed to possess.

"He'll be here," I said, hoping I meant it.

"You better get chur ass over here and get this crab boil goin'."

"There's nothing I can do until Clement gets here," I said. I saw Brook smile out of the corner of my eye. I turned to face her. She had a dimple on her left cheek, and for a moment, I thought about giving her a big ole kiss on the lips. But I thought better of it.

I heard Larue's rumble of laughter and followed his eyes to my golf cart. My forty-pound canine, known in Louisiana as a Rat-Terrier "Fiest," had plopped down on the seat of Unit #2 and tracked mud everywhere in the process.

"Turk! Git-la-blah! Zhon-di-shea! Zhon-di-shea!" He jumped up and ran off. In my peripheral vision, I sensed confusion and knew she was curious about my gibberish.

"French?"

"Ahh, creole, I think…, but mainly, it's Claude," I said, leaning over and cleaning the mud off with my sweat rag.

"What's Claude?"

"My grandfather."

"You are so weird."

"The dude abides," I said and climbed in. "See you at the party?"

"Of course," she said. As I drove away, she added, "Maybe you'll tell me what's up with the name of your boat?"

Toby called back as I was finishing a long hot shower. One of the advantages of my houseboat is the massive aluminum pontoons that held two thousand gallons of fresh water and a thirty-kilowatt diesel generator that ensured it was hot when I needed it to be.

"Max, what's goin' on, my friend," Toby said in his distinct, sharp cadence that reminded me of an old-school football coach. The one that walks around with an extra chin strap and raps you on the helmet with it when you get out of line. *BIINNGG!*

"Thanks for calling back, Compadre."

"No sweat. Man, I wish I had some better news. Be good to catch up, you know?"

"I hear ya, Bro. Soon, man, soon. Alright…, let's hear it."

"He was one of three prisoners the State was taking to Jackson for treatment of some kind. There was a struggle, and their van ran off the road and hit a tree. Three dead guards and two dead prisoners - no Donnie."

"Jesus… Treatment for what?"

"I don't know…," Toby said in a manner that meant he didn't care. I guess they think the last two years of his condemned life need to be "quality. "All I know is somebody over here in Mississippi shit the bed. They're sending me and some other guys from Texas to relieve the team there now."

"That's good news," I thought. Should this escalate and I need to get involved, having someone who can help me instead of someone I must evade and circumvent will be much easier.

"What about Jennifer Tyner? Did he kill her?"

"We're still gathering evidence, but his tracks end at the river's edge. If you ask me…"

He didn't need to continue. "Yep," I said, "If it looks like a duck, walks like a duck, and quacks…"

"It's a duck," Toby finished the riddle.

"And a flock of mallards is working the decoys."

"Max, that ain't all," Toby said. That is the second worst thing someone can say to me, followed by, "We need to talk." An added abhorrence is the necessity for a response.

"Proceed."

"A body was found a few hours ago in Natchez mashed against a concrete barrier, bobbing in the current near one of the gambling boats."

"Who, Toby?"

"Amy Dews."

My chest felt heavy as I hustled to the table and looked at the atlas. Greenville, Natchez… when I didn't respond, Toby said, "Max?"

"Miller is next," I said.

"What's that?"

"Miller Toussaint," I repeated. "One of my group from that night. Donnie is going downriver, picking us off one by one geographically. But how in hell would he find out where everyone lives?" I asked.

Being in the business of prisoners, Toby said, "Dude, you have no idea what these guys can get their hands on. Nowadays, even somewhere as backwoods as Mississippi, they have computers and Wi-Fi. Privileges are extended to members of The Red Hat Gang (death row members)."

"I don't even think Donnie can read. You know the stereotype about backwoods people diddling their sisters?" I said rhetorically. "Donnie is about a one-third a chromosome away from licking windows."

"You'd be surprised what a highly motivated individual can accomplish with enough time and the right opportunity."

"I suppose. Well, that settles it. Looks like I'm headed that way also."

"Max, I can't have you going all 00-Redneck on me."

"Toby, my Cajun Compadre…, whatever are you suggesting?"

"Aight, but you gotta do what I tell you, you. Next thing I know, you'll have Specter Gunships strafing the Port of New Orleans." In the Cajun dialect, the words flowed, *the Porta a Nawlins*

"I'll take that as a compliment."

"It's not when it's regarding an escaped death row inmate – who's recently become my responsibility," said Deputy US Marshal Toby Guillory.

Things were slow with the private security firm I ran with my mentor, James Sims, former head of the CIA's Special Activities Division. The nature of the business is things are quiet until they aren't. The schedule is that of a smokejumper. Like I'd told Hegar, my other job, co-host of a syndicated fishing show, was on hiatus until February. My partner, Jeb, could handle anything in that regard. It meant I was free to deal with the problem at hand.

When Clement arrived, I'd let him know we'd be flying out first thing. That may be a problem, depending on when he starts drinking.

DEAD RIVER

What if the epicenter of the Covid pandemic wasn't Wuhan, China, but Fort Myers, Florida, and the symptoms weren't "flu like" but were neurological? Imagine the carnage should sixty percent of the population be under varying degrees of psychosis. When a virus spawned from the toxic blue-green algae bloom in the form of a neurotoxin, the Upper Caloosahatchee Waterway became a

DEAD RIVER.

DEAD RIVER

Patient A'hole

Tallahassee, Florida
March 15ᵗʰ, 2019

Dr. Aimé Pinder, leading authority with the NCCOS, the agency that monitors the red tide and blue-green algae blooms in Florida, along with representatives of MOTE Marine Laboratory in Sarasota, stood before the Florida Senate and stated the facts. "Sir, please heed my warning that there has been a mutation within the bacteria found in cyanobacteria, identical to what has taken over much of the Upper Caloosahatchee Waterway. Not Karenia brevis (red tide), which predominantly occurs in saltwater environments, but the blue-green algae that the US Corps of Engineers is pumping out of Lake Okeechobee."

"What kind of mutation, Doctor?" asked Senator White, a proponent of the Clean Water Act spearheaded by a sportsman's foundation known as Captain's For Clean Water.

"Well, Mr. White, from what we can tell at this point, the symptoms in humans might not be exclusive to respiratory, like in the past, but the new bacteria chain suggests the effects could be…, well, mental."

The chamber erupted in chatter until incumbent Governor Breen called to order and said, "Dr. Pinder, what evidence do you have to back this up?"

"Well, Sir, the data suggests…." Aimé began but was interrupted by the Governor.

"The data suggests… Dr. Pinder, what are you saying? People should avoid the river because they might go crazy?"

"Yes, Sir," Dr. Pinder responded.

"Do you know what that will do to the economy of Florida?"

"I do, Sir. That said, I'm not sure if you understand the alternative."

Caloosahatchee River – Eastern Fort Myers, Florida July 16, 2019

Barry Hengle was a wormy little shit who dyed his hair jet black and always had a cigar hanging out of his mouth. No matter how hard he tried, he couldn't help but look like a sixty-five-year-old version of Alfred E. Newman with more prominent ears. If there were a pyramid of biblical proportion, built entirety of assholes, Barry would be the pinnacle.

The bartenders breathed a sigh of relief when he left the Boat House Restaurant at 10 pm, as they did every Thursday night when the miserable regular would grace them with his presence in his little jon-boat. The wind had died, leaving the summer air still and stagnant, sticky. His head was pounding, as it had been all day. Headaches were something he lived with, but these were different to the point that Barry considered re-considering his stance on the possible neurological issues associated with the toxicity of the blue-green algae that had consumed the Upper Caloosahatchee Waterway.

The river looked more like the fairway of a finely manicured golf course, a dense mat of green as far as the eye could see. Controversy had been widespread about the water that the Army Corps of Engineers released annually from Lake Okeechobee into the Caloosahatchee and other tidal waterways. Barry was one of many who chose to ignore the science associated with the agricultural industry pollutants contaminating the lake. His buddies kept telling him what was causing these headaches, but Barry considered this problem more ecological, not neurological.

Barry had gone to the public hearing because of the impacts on his marine construction business. He was hoping to hear good news, not listen to some uppity Bahamian doctor lecture about chemistry. Not to mention his Dudley-DO-Right neighbor, Jeb Copeland, big-shot TV personality– always harping on pollution this and pollution that - making it increasingly difficult for Barry to obtain permits for building in environmentally sensitive areas.

Barry idled away from the dock, turned starboard, and punched the throttle. Overcast moonlight reflected off the green sheen, and the wind offered no relief from the warm river. About a mile upriver, his motor began to sputter, then it coughed and died. *Jesus H Christ on a popsicle stick …Not mechanical problems, please.* Then it occurred to Barry that he couldn't remember when he'd put fuel in the boat. *They generally don't run without a source of combustion, you idiot.* He shook the gas can, low but not empty.

Good for Barry; he'd never owned a boat without a bow-mounted trolling motor. He took a powerful headlamp out of the console, fit it over his elephant ears, and turned it on, illuminating the water's surface – a sickening bluish-green color. He could only hope his batteries had enough juice to withstand the strain they would receive.

The moon was full, yet the dense and slow-moving clouds kept it in an intermittent haze. He turned off the headlamp so that his eyes could re-adjust to the darkness. He stepped onto the deck while pulling back on a cord that released the trolling motor, letting it go when the foot reached over the bow and into the water. The bracket *clicked* as the closure snapped around the pin. Barry turned the handle clockwise as far as it would go. The aluminum boat jolted forward in response to the twenty-four pounds of thrust pulling it.

Fog hovered off the surface in an eerie fashion as the trolling motor cut a swath through the sludge.

Barry wasn't scared, but something didn't seem right. He had a strange feeling he had stumbled upon something private. It seemed as if eyes were watching him, lurking through the mangroves and from behind the docks, weathered and beaten from last year's hurricane.

Upon turning the headlamp back on and looking around, he could see that he was on a stretch of the river barren of development, just pastures, a grassy bank, cattails, and mangroves. Barry began to traverse diagonally across towards the seawall, considering the possibility of his batteries dying and leaving him adrift, stranded in and amongst the links of Blue-Green Algae that had become the upper portion of the river. Being able to reach the shore would at least give him some options.

Barry pressed his thumb into the bridge of his nose to ease the pain in his throbbing head. Although the relief was brief, like a metronome pumping shards of glass into his head.

with each heartbeat, *throb, throb, throb*. He looked around the dead river—no one in sight, no current swirls, no signs of sea life, nothing. He and the insects were seemingly the only living beings. The only sound was the trolling motor lapping at the brackish water and algae mix.

But in an instant, there was no sound at all. The batteries had died. Usually, this would have been a gradual process, not an immediate loss of power. Yet this was just the beginning of the odd chain of events unfolding around him.

Luckily, his momentum carried him close enough to grab a dock, pull himself in, and tie off to the dock cleat. The smell of the contaminated and possibly toxic river was foul, and he felt the urge to hold his nose as he took the mosquito suit out of his gear bag and pulled it on. Sweat immediately began to accumulate, trapped inside the extra layer.

All he could think about was lying down and trying to ease the pain in his head. He could spend the rest of the night, walk to the nearest house in the morning, and get help. *"Shit...,"* Barry remembered the Caribbean cruise he'd booked months ago. He could only hope he'd get home in time.

Barry tossed some life jackets around to assemble a makeshift pallet. They were the orange USCG type II ones strapped around the tourists who rented pontoon boats at marinas along the coast.

Barry thought he saw a figure dart from the cattails and into the backyard next door. *Jesus, was that a Chupacabra? My mind is playing tricks on me.* Focusing was nearly impossible. The pain had moved from his forehead to behind his eyes and had become excruciating.

Lying down on his side, Barry pulled the mesh hood of his mosquito suit over his face and laid his head against one of the life preservers. Through the mesh, he watched the clouds move slowly across the moon in streaks of yellowish-grey.

Barry's next memory was waking up in the boat, sweating, the sun in his eyes. His headache was gone, but he felt hungover even though he'd only had a couple beers. There was a light breeze, and a current had returned, moving the tablecloth of green algae downriver like a massive toxic barge.

He sat up to find a trail of bloody footprints leading from the bow to where he lay, oblivious to the gore on his face, especially around his mouth. He felt around his body for injuries; there were none.

The tide was out, and with 3–5-foot tidal movement combined with Barry's short stature, the dock was well over his head. As he stepped onto the bow to see where the footprints led, he noticed a red cord in the corner of the boat – the killswitch, a rudimentary safety device that shuts off the motor should the operator become separated from the helm. *I'll be damned. I must've pulled it loose last night. Huh... Weird*, Barry thought in that he never wore the thing.

Barry, a textbook hedonist, forgot about the implications of his scenario and focused on making the trip to the Port of Tampa to catch his cruise. He fit the prong end of the killswitch behind the button on the outboard, allowing fuel to reach the motor. After pumping the bubble on the fuel line, he turned the key. The engine sputtered a couple of times and then fired.

Barry untied from the dock, preoccupied and riddled with anxiety. Had he not found the nature of his "engine trouble," he would have noticed the bloody mess on the dock and the body underneath held against the understructure by the incoming water.

Blowing through a Slow Speed Manatee Zone, he ran on plane through the bay and up the canal leading to his house, his wake rocking everything in its path. He docked his boat, ran inside, shed his clothes, and jumped in the shower without looking in the mirror. Still feeling like hammered dog shit, Barry got out of the door just in time to make the two-and-a-half-hour drive to the Port of Tampa.

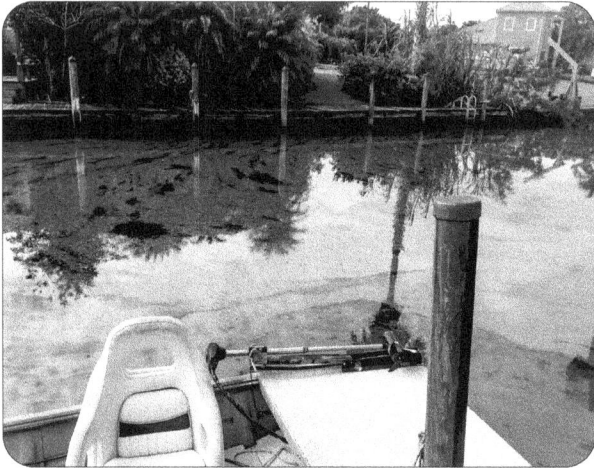

2

Dead River

Upper Caloosahatchee Waterway –
Eastern Fort Myers, Florida
July 16th, 2019

Jeb Copeland was outside spraying a reddish pollen-like substance off his center-console fishing boat when Tom, his next-door neighbor, one door removed, came tipping down the narrow concrete seawall like a kitty cat all nimbly-bimbly from limb to limb. This isn't saying much for Kitty, Jeb's overweight grey tabby, but for a seawall-balancing sixty-year-old man, it is.

"Hey there, Jeb," Tom said, reaching the end of the seawall and hopping onto the dock. "What chu duin'?"

"Spraying this shit off my boat," Jeb told him as he watched it fall into the water, where it left an oily ring before disintegrating into the air. The stench was gone. The taste of metal on your tongue wasn't, nor was the *tickle* in the back of your throat.

The outdoor duties were out of habit, as no one was going out during the worst red tide blooms in the region's history. Whether or not the red tide coincides with the blue-green algae that had taken over the river is a topic of scientific discussion. The effects of both naturally occurring events on humans is a broader subject, one not much publicized. The miles upon miles of dead fish polluting the coastline was terrible enough; no one wanted to further the negative publicity. Albeit, trying to hide it now is as apparent as the comb-over for the balding guy.

"Thought you might be getting ready to do another fishin' show," Tom said, the excitement evident in his voice. Tom was a fisherman, as was Jeb; it just so happens that Jeb did it as the co-host of a nationally syndicated TV show, *The Adventures of Capt. Max Dean with "The Outlaw" Capt. Jeb Copeland.* Jeb's name was a recent addition, a result of lucrative contract renegotiations.

"Na," Jeb said. "The next show is out of Marathon and still a few months out. And this… I'm afraid no one is doing anything in this crap, Amigo."

"At least you can see the water," Tom said. It was true; the Army Corps of Engineers had closed the Franklin Lock, stopping the influx of the toxic blue-green algae from Lake Okeechobee, and a full moon tide flushed their canal pretty well. However, a steady west wind

brought fresh red tide. Jeb and Tom were both periodically engaged in the Red-Tide Hack, a series of short,
sharp coughs performed instinctively in response to the
lung irritation – that *tickle* I was referring to.

"I guess," Jeb said as he exited the boat, turned
off the water, and rolled the hose onto a cradle nailed to
a piling.

"They sent out a notice saying don't drink it, the
water… I don't know."

"I saw that," Jeb replied, referring to the notice
the City of Fort Myers sent to the residents of Olga and
Fort Myers Shores, warning them of possible contaminated water.

"They say it's making some people sick… I don't
know," said Tom.

"The water or the air?" Jeb wasn't concerned
about the tap water; it was the little particles dancing
around in his lungs and the headaches he found discon-
certing. "Who drinks it anyway?" Jeb asked, rubbing his
nose like it was allergy season.

"Both, I guess. I seem fine. I don't know…" Saying, "I don't know…" at the end of statements and many
times nonsensically was a verbal tick of Tom's that Jeb
and his son, Will, found nearly impossible not to laugh
at.

A biologist with the Mote Marine Laboratory in
Sarasota, Dr. Aimé Pinder, warned the Lee County Board
of County Commissioners about a potential mutation in
the algae spores that would present a problem should it
become airborne.

Jeb, sitting in the audience with Tom, several of
the local guides, and marine tradesman - including as-

shole extraordinaire himself, Barry Hengle - wasn't as quick to dismiss her as a radical environmentalist as did much of the County Board, about half of the people in attendance, including Barry, of course.

"Who drinks it anyway?" Jeb asked, rubbing his nose like it was allergy season. He spoke in starts and stops while he walked around the dock, straightening up stuff that didn't need straightening. "I was… *Kack*, coughing last night, and… *Kack*, had a headache. So, I guess, *Kack*, we'll see." It didn't take a biologist to ascertain something is amiss. The green mat covering the entire upper portion of the Caloosahatchee River was a good indication.

What do Florida red tide algae blooms and psilocybin mushrooms have in common besides being fungi? They both induce panic attacks. Jeb knew that from experience. He didn't mention to Tom that the night before, he had woken up amidst one, gasping for air as sharp waves of nervous energy surged through his body. Jeb recognized the sensation, and after a few minutes of meditation and deep breathing, he was fine.

A panic attack is terrifying the first time. It's no picnic after that, but when you have no idea what is happening, it cripples you with fear. Jeb has had four, including this one. Twice with similar scenarios following red-tide events and once when he was a freshman in high school after eating magic mushrooms for the first time. Although, he didn't realize he'd had a panic attack until later in life when he had the first "red-tide" affiliated panic attack.

After being on the water all day during a nasty red tide outbreak, he woke up out of breath, fighting for air. He thought he was having a heart attack and had his ex-wife drive him to the emergency room. When they told Jeb he was having an anxiety attack, that moment in high school came rushing back to his memory. *Holy shit… that's what happened… A panic attack.*

On the way to school, freshman year, sitting at the stop light waiting to turn left, the shrooms' had kicked in. He remembers laughing until his friend, Peanut, rolled sideways across the seat of the truck and up the window, where he proceeded to crawl onto the ceiling.

The next thing Jeb remembered was being parked somewhere and telling Peanut he had to take him home. The thing is, Jeb had been driving. One might think such a thing would be a life-long deterrent against drugs.

One thing is sure: when a weather event, or naturally occurring phenomenon (as it's called), causes some of the same behavior as a powerful hallucinogen, you might have a problem. Can you imagine a large portion of the population tripping at one time?

Tom stood at the fish cleaning table facing the canal on the bay side, opening into the river. He was fidgeting with his hands, rubbing them together, mainly the left over the right, which was no "tick." Several months prior, Jeb took Tom fishing in the 10,000 Islands, where Tom was impaled by a saltwater catfish, worse than Jeb had ever seen anyone impaled, dorsal fin entirely through his right palm.

"Hand still bothering you?" Jeb asked. "You ok, Amigo?" It was clear he wasn't. "Got something on your mind?"

Returning to the here and now, Tom said, "Oh, I don't know. I was just thinking about the lady that got murdered downriver."

"What?" Jeb looked up quizzically, as this was news to him.

"Well, shoot, some lady downriver got murdered, so they say… I don't know. It was just on the news."

"Got any more details than that, Bubba?" Jeb asked. It's not uncommon for Jeb to call people he likes "Bubba."

"Just that they found her out by the pool, mutilated, they say. Haven't found who done it yet. I don't know."

A memory of something seemingly insignificant hit Jeb like a weighted billy club. There was something about peeing outside that Jeb found freeing. He never peed indoors if there was an outdoor option. That said, outside one's "options" are relative, leaving Jeb a wide range to piss freely. Which is what he was doing sometime before daylight when he saw their neighbor, Barry Hengle, come idling in.

"Follow me," Jeb said and hurried down the seawall to the cul-de-sac of the canal and up the other side to the third house – directly across from Tom's. Jeb spoke along the way, Tom fast behind him, "I saw Barry come idling in sometime before daybreak. I remembered thinking something was strange, but I was half asleep, and considering that something is always "off" with that dude, I thought nothing of it. Until you said something."

No one in the neighborhood was particularly fond of him. He and Jeb had a blow-up one time – once. Barry is one of those guys who's not used to being called out for being an asshole. Those people usually fall in line once confronted with equal or superior assholeism.

Jeb found peace with his inner asshole long ago; they have a good relationship - he's there when Jeb needs him. The first time Barry got sideways with Jeb was the last. It didn't stop the looks, or the frivolous complaints filed by "anonymous" neighbors, just the rants that he subjected most of everyone else to.

As they neared Barry's house, Jeb walked to the street to find the man's truck gone. "He's gone," Jeb said in a loud whisper for some reason as he jogged back to Barry's dock.

"Oh, man…" Tom said as they stood on the dock looking down into Barry's little skiff. There was blood everywhere. Something caught Tom's eye, and impulsively, he jumped in the boat.

"Hey, Man. Get out of there. What are you doing, Dude? That's a crime scene."

"Oh, shoot," Tom said. "holding up what appeared to be a piece of women's clothing. "Is cross-dressing a fetish of Barry's, or is it a clue?"

"Be careful and don't disturb anything, and for God's sake, don't touch that blood."

"Aww, shoot," Tom replied, looking at the red crust on the bottom of his palm resting on the console.

Jeb took his phone from the waistband of his board shorts and dialed 911.

Ten minutes later, a plain-clothes detective with a flat-top haircut and a chiseled chin walked through the front yard with an outstretched hand. "Detective Billy Hawkins - Lee County Sheriff's Department." Jeb introduced himself, and they shook hands. Hawkins's grip was firm, and he made direct eye contact.

Upon seeing the boat and listening to their story, Hawkins called in the Crime Scene Unit. Hawkins talked to Tom while we waited, as he had a lot to say, nearly crawling out of his skin with anxiety over possibly disturbing the scene.

A few minutes later, CSI arrived. As Tom spoke to them, Jeb told Detective Hawkins about seeing Barry idling in early this morning, looking more agitated and disheveled than usual.

"Didn't look right?" Hawkins repeated what Jeb said in a way that meant elaborate.

"Look," said Jeb, "Barry is a peculiar guy, physically and personally. No one in the neighborhood gets along with him – classic bipolar if you ask me, causing scenes over silly things, hollering at everyone. That's why I thought nothing of it until Tom mentioned the murder. Then we came over here and found this," I said, motioning to Barry's boat.

"Any idea where he might be?"

"No idea," Jeb said as his phone rang. It was Jeb's son, Will, who was on a cruise that left Houston earlier that morning with the former Mrs. Copeland and Jeb's husband-in-law, Dwayne, also her former boss. It's funny how things work out that way. "I need to take this," Jeb said and excused himself.

"Hey, Bub. How's the Three-Hour-Tour?" Jeb asked, knowing my son wouldn't get the Gilligan's Island reference.

"It's fine," Will said. "Mom goes to the gym for several hours, then hits the pool." For Will's mom, "pool" was code for "vodka." "Dwayne follows her around with the piss bucket as always."

"Be nice," Jeb said, although he had no respect for the man. When it came to Will, Dwayne was nothing more than a sounding board for his wife. No matter the issue, he sided with her, which to Jeb, was chicken shit.

"This dude with big ears caused a scene in the dining room a few hours after we left Tampa. We were eating lunch, and they had to remove him – drunk or went nuts or something. I got it on video. Here, I just sent it to you."

"Maybe he and your mother should get together," Jeb laughed. He did his best not to disparage the boy's mother – too much. Hell, he didn't care that she drank, nor did he think she had a problem. Jeb knows people with drinking problems; their lives are unmanageable. So far, Rhonda was managing just fine.

"I better run, Bub. Tom and I are outside doing something." Jeb didn't see the point in mentioning what was going on.

"Ok, Dad. Tell Tom I said hey."

"Will do. Later."

As Jeb returned to the scene, he opened the video Will sent. It stopped him in his tracks. The man Will referred to was short and skinny with jet-black hair and huge ears – Barry Hengle. If not for the appearance, his voice was distinctive, that primal yell. It was him, alright. Jeb completed the few remaining steps and stood amidst the group, mouth agape.

"What's a matter there, Jeb," Tom said. "You look like you seen a ghost."

"I know where Barry Hengle is," Jeb said and showed them the video.

Hawkins immediately got on the phone to relay the information while the crime scene unit finished up. Afterward, the Detective handed Jeb his card and said he'd be in touch.

"Should I tell my son there's a murderer on board?"

"I'd hold off for a little while," Hawkins said. "We need to confirm a few things."

Holding his card, Jeb dialed his number. When Hawkins answered, Jeb said, "There's my number. Please call me as soon as you know something. My kid is aboard that ship."

"You got it."

It was nearly two o'clock when they finished talking to Hawkins. The summer sun was high in the Southwest Florida sky, the air was still and dense, and Jeb was pouring with sweat. Although born and raised in the southern heat, Jeb never became accustomed to it. He went inside to towel off, cool down, and hydrate before preparing material for the next TV show scheduled to shoot in two months out of Marathon Key. Jeb had no idea that producing a fishing show would be so much work. But he loved it.

A desk in the shape of a right triangle sat in a corner of his bedroom with windows facing the water. Just weeks ago, wild parrots flushed from thatches of palms and snook murdered baitfish in the canal with loud *gulp-pops*! Birds of all kinds sang in every direction, and manatees lumbered to and fro. Now, everything just seemed dead.

The hours flew by like flushed quail. At magic hour, one hour before sunset, Jeb took his laptop and moved to the back porch, which faced west, not a bad view in SWFL. But lately, the condition of the river, the red tide, and the general state of the environment had fucked with his serenity. The sun fell beyond the tops of the furthest palm trees, and he watched it bleed into a doomed horizon.

At twilight, he turned on the patio lights and went inside to pre-heat the oven – 400 degrees. Jeb's cat, he called her Kitty, trotted in from somewhere, meowing in broken-breathed meows, and launched her considerable mass onto the sink, crashing into the cabinets as she went. Jeb looked around at the dirty paw prints that lay waste in the lower kitchen cabinets.

"Dammit, Kitty, why do you insist on making me jump through hoops?"

"MEOW," she said and turned back to the faucet.

"You have fresh water. You know that I know that you do."

She motioned to the faucet again, "Meow. Meow, meow, meow…"

"Ok, ok," Jeb said, taking the frozen DiGiorno pizza from the freezer and tossing it on the counter. He walked to the sink and turned on the faucet as the pre-heat buzzer buzzed.

Kitty reached her paw into the stream. "Meow?"

"Good God almighty," he said, tapping the pressure down.

Jeb jumped in the shower, shaved, and wrapped his evening sarong around his waist in time to take his dinner out of the oven. *I've got to start eating better,* he thought, cutting the pizza into squares with a Dexter fillet knife.

Taking the pizza and two water bottles outside, Jeb began reviewing footage for the latest *Adventure of the Saltwater Cowboys*, *"Beavertail Sandwich,"* airing later in the month. This one was going to be epic, as an eleven-foot gator commenced to chomping the gunnel of a brand new skiff on loan from a sponsor.

3

Nightmare in Olga

Upper Caloosahatchee Waterway –
Eastern Fort Myers, Florida
Evening, July 16th - Early Morning, July 17th, 2019

Jeb was wrapping up his work for the evening, moving from the back patio back inside, when a loud *"Crash"* rang out. He jumped up to investigate and heard the first gunshot. *BOOM! Shotgun, Twelve-gauge, heavy loads.* Changing direction, he hustled to his bedroom, removed his Sig 229 .40 caliber from the gun safe, racked a round into the chamber, and ran outside.

Some neighbors tipped nervously around their lawns, trying to get a look. While others, including Mrs. Patton, Jeb's old bag pain in the ass, next-door neighbor -

opposite side of Tom, rubbernecked out of windows and half-cracked doors.

"Jeb… Jeb," she said with her pudgy face mashed into a small crack in her front door. He could barely hear over what he could only describe as "maniacal rants" happening three blocks down on the opposite side of the street.

"Get back inside and call the police," Jeb said. Mrs. Patton's mouth moved, but it was just a hole moving around a canvas of flesh.

Goddammit... In the melee, Jeb forgot about his "evening sarong" that flapped against his legs as he ran to the storm ditch, duckwalking to within forty yards of the accident, where he lay on the grass and looked onto the street.

A minivan t-boned a RAM 150 Pickup Truck at the intersection. It was nonsensical in that the street ended at River Forrest Drive, and there was nowhere for the T-boner to go: ditch, yard, house, then canal. More notable was the woman who stood beside the minivan looking down the barrel of a still smoking twelve gauge. Jeb watched the smoke rising from it in the dull streetlight and followed the woman's gaze to a body lying in a heap near the busted grill of the RAM.

Close-range headshot, face completely scooped out, no blood on the grill nor on the pavement that Jeb could see. Indicating the victim's blood, skin, bone, and brains were blown into the ether like a clay pigeon powdered in a skeet shooting contest.

The lady moved the shotgun to a woman who had escaped the wrecked RAM pickup. Hands up in a submissive manner, crying, she begged the shotgun-wielding woman for her life. With no other play, Jeb ran into the street, gun up. "Drop it!"

When she turned in his direction, Jeb had never seen eyes that penetrating and realized he was dealing with something more sinister than he could have imagined. He hesitated, and it nearly cost him his life.

Boom! She fired. Jeb heard the BBs passing overhead as he dove into the swale. His sarong had come undone in the melee and desperately needed readjustment. More screams turned his direction overhead. *Boom!* She fired again.

The pleading lady had used the diversion to make a run for it, but Minivan Lady cut her down in the process. Jeb had a decision to make. Run into the street naked as a jay-bird and end this lickity-split, or take a second to cover himself and hope he had enough time before she got a bead on him. Jeb chose the former and sprinted to the other side of the street, flanking her. "Drop your weapon! Now!"

Hyper-alert, she swung the shotgun in Jeb's direction. He was ready this time. *Bang!* Her head snapped back, and she collapsed as the .40 caliber hollow point bullet peeled off the back of her skull. A chunk stuck to the side of the minivan and slid down. Jeb placed the Sig on the ground, picked up the sarong, and covered himself. Jeb's neighbors began to trickle out of their homes, and he wondered how many saw him in all his glory. *Fuck it...* Jeb thought as he walked home. From behind, Jeb heard Mrs. Patton blathering, "Well... uh... wait a minute, Jeb. Where are you going?"

"To put some pants on and check on Tom. Have you called 911?"

"Yes, but the Sheriff's Department told me they were inundated with calls and to stay inside and remain calm until further notice."

"OK. Then, wait on the police. Tell them what happened if they get here before I get back."

"Jeb, I don't know what happened. What is happening?"

Jeb told the truth, "I don't know," and ran home. He threw on jeans and a T-shirt, stepped into some flip-flops, shoved the pistol in the back of his waistband, and ran through the patio to Tom's.

He knocked on the door and looked through the windows, nothing. He hollered, "Tom! Hey, Tom! You in there, Amigo?" No response. Jeb walked around the side of the garage to find the door open. "Tom? You in here, Buddy?" Jeb asked and walked in slowly. He could hear somebody; it was pitch black otherwise. "Tom?" Jeb asked again, reaching for the light switch.

Tom was standing at his workbench with his back to Jeb, wearing nothing but white tube socks. "Well… I don't know. I think I bout got that hardhead fin out of my hand," he said.

"What's that, Tom?" He must have been dreaming about the catfish sting he'd gotten weeks ago in the 10,000 Islands. There couldn't have been remains from the saltwater cat, or else his hand would have gotten infected long ago. The pain was seared into his mind because when he turned around, Jeb saw that he'd cut all of the meat out of his left palm and stacked it in a neat, bloody pile.

"Tom, listen to me, Buddy. You're sick. I'm gonna get you some help. Why don't we go inside and try to dress that up?" However, even with Jeb's training, all he could have done was pack it and control the bleeding.

Tom looked down, started laughing, and grabbed the head of his prick.

"Tom, what are you doing." Jeb began walking forward as he took a pair of lawn shears from the bench. "Tom! Put those shears down!" Tom pulled his taffy taut, opened the shears wide, and as Jeb yelled, "Tom! Don't!" snipped it off.

"Well, I don't know... guess I won't be needing that no more," he said, tossing his hacked Johnson towards the waste can in the corner. It hit the side and bounced out, landing on the floor with a flat *thud.* He fell over onto the cold slab, blood pooling around him.

Jeb snatched some towels from a cabinet and rushed to his friend, "Tom, we've got to hold pressure on that, or you're going to bleed out." Tom scooted away surprisingly fast when Jeb tried to get close. Then he heard a commotion outside, the squelch of radios, and ran out of the garage to the front of the house.

The police had arrived; Jeb could see lights shining around his house. "Hey! Over here! Man down!" Jeb hollered and ran back to the garage to find Tom in the fetal position, the blood pool steadily growing in an even radius around him. After a few moments, Jeb ran to the front of the house to find two Lee County Sheriff's Deputies creeping from his yard toward Tom's with their guns drawn.

"Over here!" Jeb yelled. "Man down!"

As they approached, Jeb could see they were taking no chances. They must've thought he had killed the people at the intersection. *Where the hell was Mrs. Pat-*

ton? They descended with speed and aggression. "Keep your hands where we can see them!"

Holding up his hands, Jeb said loud enough for them to hear, "Did you talk to my neighbor? Did she not tell you what happened?"

"Slowly remove the gun and lay it on the ground in front of you!" screamed the lead officer.

Jeb took his gun from the back of his jeans and placed it on the driveway.

"Step back! Clasp your fingers behind your head and put your face in the pavement!"

Complying, Jeb said, "My neighbor, Tom…, he just… he just…, he cut his dick off, man! He's bleeding out in there!"

The officer in control knelt on Jeb's back, digging his knee in real good as he handcuffed him. "Hey, Man! Now you're pissing me off! Ask my neighbor, Mrs. Patton. She'll confirm what I said."

He dug his knee in harder. "Shut up! Stop resisting!"

"My friend is dying in there, you fucking idiot!" Jeb turned my head to see the other officer standing there perplexedly. "You just gonna stand there? My friend is in there dying, you dumb fuck!"

The knee again. "Dude! Dude, I'm gonna tell you one more time." Jeb was mad as a hornet, his redneck blood boiling, a dull *hum* in his ears.

Through the blinding crime scene lights up the street, he saw Detective Hawkins working his way toward Tom's.

"What the fuck are you doing?" Hawkins asked the cop who was on top of Jeb as he approached. "Haynes! Get the fuck off of him right now."

"This guy was involved in the shooting!" Haynes replied. Jeb bucked, throwing Haynes off balance. He had good reflexes and recovered, coming down on Jeb harder.

Hawkins slapped him across his head with an open palm, knocking his cap off. Haynes rolled onto the driveway, holding his head. "What the fuck, Hawkins!"

"I told you to get up," Hawkins said as he removed the handcuffs and helped Jeb to his feet.

Jeb jumped up and got in the second officer's face. "You chicken shit motherfucker…" and shoved him.

"Hold up, Jeb," Hawkins said, putting his hand on Jeb's shoulder.

"Tom is in there dying, Bro!" Jeb yelled and ran to the garage.

Hawkins put his pinkies in his mouth, whistled the loudest whistle you've ever heard, and screamed, "Medic!"

Inside the garage, Jeb felt for a pulse – nothing. From the doorway, Hawkins asked, "Dead?"

"Yep. Probably because of those morons out there," Jeb said, pretty sure that Tom wouldn't be dead if he'd gotten help sooner.

Kneeing at the body, Hawkins said, "Holy shit…. Did he?"

"Indeed, he did. I watched him do it. Then he tossed it at the trash can like a wad of paper. See?" Jeb motioned to the dismembered member.

"Jesus," Hawkins said as the medics ran into the garage with a stretcher. Hawkins looked at them, shaking his head. Jeb had no reply.

Hawkins and Jeb left Tom's and made their way back to the scene of the accident. Jeb smelled smoke from a nearby fire. It occurred to him that he'd been in less chaotic war zones. He could see Hawkins shaking his head knowingly.

"What?"

" Special forces?"

"How'd you know?" Jeb asked, although reasonably sure he knew the answer. Hawkins had that aura about him, and it was not difficult for members of the Special Forces Community to spot each other.

"I had a feeling. But now…" Hawkins said, looking around at the scene, "There's no other explanation, no good one anyway. 75th Ranger Regiment. You?"

"Air Force. 24th Special Tactics."

"Whoa… Tier 1," Hawkins said in "mock" respect.

Jeb shrugged modestly and said, "That was a long time ago."

The US groups the Special Forces into three tiers. Tier 3 is for large, conventional warfare units. Tier 2 comprises Special Operations Forces, including the SEAL Teams (besides Team 6) and Army Rangers (Detective Hawkins).

Tier 1 operators are the most elite soldiers in the world. The "All Stars" of the Joint Special Operations Command include DEVGRU (Seal Team 6), 1st Special Forces Operational Detachment Delta – Delta Force,

Army Intelligence, and 24th Special Tactics Squadron – Jeb's unit.

An Air Force Combat Controller, Jeb is trained like other Tier 1 operators, except he is also qualified to control air traffic. In Jeb's case, that meant calling in close air support and painting targets for bombs in the Tora Bora Mountain Range.

A clamor from a crowd of uniformed deputies caught their attention from the coroners loading the bodies into the ambulances. "That's Jeb, the one I was telling you about!" Mrs. Patten yelled and waddled towards Jeb and Detective Hawkins with mussed hair.

"Afraid you missed the first patrol, didn't you there?" Jeb said as sarcastically as he could, having gone through the wringer, presumably due to Mrs. Patton's lack of a backbone.

"I… I… I got scared, Jeb. I'm sorry."

Feeling bad, Jeb replied, "It's ok. Go on home now. I'll come check on you in a minute." She wobbled off, mumbling something.

Out of the blue, Hawkins said, "I'll be damned. I didn't peg *"The Outlaw"* for a military man."

"So you watch the show?" Before syndication, Jeb was only noticed regionally in certain circles. Afterward, his notoriety soared.

"Of course. I'm a fisherman. Dude, you were hilarious in that last episode."

"*Lookin' a Little Green*?" Jeb asked.

"That's the one."

"Thanks, Man," Jeb said, "I appreciate that."

Hawkins shifted his weight from leg to leg like those with knee pain often do. "So, is it true what they say about Max?" he asked of Jeb's co-host, referring to the rumors, stories, and lore that he was some black-ops super spy. With a crooked grin, he added, "You would know."

Hawkins, a Special Forces Operator himself, was aware of the Tier structure and how it relates to special missions. The CIA conducts the most secretive missions, usually led by a paramilitary operator from their "ultra-secretive" Special Activities Division - the types of people capable of doing what it is said Max does. Hawkins knew it, as well as the standard of each team having one assigned Air Force CCT (Combat Controller).

"What? *Pppfff*... No, that's bullshit," Jeb white lied, rubbing his wrist from where the cuffs had dug in. Changing the topic, Jeb asked, "Any idea what's going on here?"

Hawkins took a deep breath. "They're saying some kind of viral outbreak, like meningitis or something."

"Who is?"

"Lee County Crisis Management."

"A viral outbreak causing psychological shit? From the algae bloom?" Jeb asked. Hawkins shrugged. Jeb's mind went to Will and the situation on the cruise ship. "Hengle."

"What about him?"

"Is there a connection here?" Jeb asked, referring to the scene at the intersection.

"There is," Hawkins said. "The mini-van lady you took out was the daughter of the woman who was found murdered earlier this morning. She, the daughter, found the body."

"The same woman my neighbor… the one currently on the same cruise ship as my son, murdered?"

"All signs point to…" Hawkins replied.

Recalling some data he'd learned during biological/chemical warfare training, Jeb said, "Depending on how the virus is transmitted, if she contracted it, that could explain it. I'm telling you, Amigo, these two instances here are nothing short of insanity. Tom," Jeb said, getting emotional, "He was the most stable person I knew." A moment passed before Jeb said, "Tom touched the blood."

"What's that?" Hawkins asked.

"Remember earlier, Tom told CSI that he'd accidentally touched some of the blood when he got in Barry's boat?" Jeb could see Hawkins' mind turning. "Is this the only instance?"

"Negative; there are a few along the river just as bizarre," Hawkins replied. They had moved to the street in front of Jeb's house when they heard a motor revving and saw bright headlights barreling down River Forest Drive—a sedan of some sort blowing through stop signs with no indications of stopping.

The EMTs and other police who had arrived began yelling and waving their hands. The ones still in the street dove out of the way at the last minute before the sedan crashed into the RAM pickup. The driver backed up, put the car in drive, and drove carefully around the wreckage. Hawkins and Jeb looked at each other in disbelief as the driver stomped the pedal. The tires squealed, and the car accelerated down the street once again.

Jeb and Hawkins watched as the car careered down the dead-end road toward a steel barricade that separated it from the river. They ran to the center of the street as it smashed into it, flipping over and crashing into the rip-rap below before rolling into the dead river.

As the first responders ran towards the scene, Jeb grabbed Hawkins by the arm and said, "Whoever is in that car, if they're not dead, they will be. This is related to Barry Hengle, I know in my gut, and the motherfucker is on the same goddamn boat as my boy."

"Go! Get out of here!" Hawkins hollered and ran towards the carnage.

Hawkins' hunch was correct; Max was the point man on two of Jeb's missions. Jeb could've said the stories weren't true and not have been lying, most of them falling short, the truth being more spectacular. He couldn't tell Hawkins that he had to reach Max right away, that he might be able to make sense of things—the only person who could help Jeb get his son.

www.ingramcontent.com/pod-product-compliance
Lightning Source LLC
Chambersburg PA
CBHW052016030426
42335CB00026B/3171